Critical Thinking

Critical Thinking

Tools for Evaluating Research

Peter M. Nardi

UNIVERSITY OF CALIFORNIA PRESS

University of California Press, one of the most
distinguished university presses in the United States,
enriches lives around the world by advancing scholarship
in the humanities, social sciences, and natural sciences. Its
activities are supported by the UC Press Foundation and
by philanthropic contributions from individuals and
institutions. For more information, visit www.ucpress.edu.

University of California Press
Oakland, California

Library of Congress Cataloging-in-Publication Data

Names: Nardi, Peter M., author.
Title: Critical thinking : tools for evaluating research /
    Peter M. Nardi.
Description: Oakland, California : University of
    California Press, [2017] | Includes bibliographical
    references and index.
Identifiers: LCCN 2017001710 (print) | LCCN 2017006808
    (ebook) | ISBN 9780520291843 (pbk. : alk. paper) |
    ISBN 9780520965478 ()
Subjects: LCSH: Critical thinking.
Classification: LCC B809.2 .N37 2017 (print) |
    LCC B809.2 (ebook) | DDC 160—dc23
LC record available at https://lccn.loc.gov/2017001710

Manufactured in the United States of America

24 23 22 21 20 19 18 17
10 9 8 7 6 5 4 3 2 1

Contents

Acknowledgments

Seth Dobrin has been a terrific editor, cold-calling me to see if I were interested in writing something for the University of California Press, shepherding this project from the start, seeking reviewers, and providing supportive feedback and comments. Thanks to Editorial Assistant Renée Donovan, Project Editor Cindy Fulton, Marketing Manager Chris Loomis, and Copy Editor Paul Psoinos for superbly overseeing the project and contributing to making this book possible (with the usual caveat that I'm the one ultimately responsible for the content should there be any errors). And to Jeff Chernin, who continues, now and forever, to provide all that critically matters.

Introduction

Critical Thinking

"Good News! Drinking Wine Before Bedtime Can Help You Lose Weight." For several years, this headline and similar postings have appeared on Twitter, Facebook, and various blogs, excitedly spreading the results of a study supposedly supporting this claim (LaCapria, 2016). Despite secretly hoping that this might be true and blindly accepting it as fact, skeptical readers should instead dig deeper than the sensational headlines and critically ask important questions about the research design. Many media outlets touting the alleged findings cited only a tabloid newspaper article written in London about four women who told anecdotes about their wine consumption and weight loss. Yet, others also reported in a few sentences the results of an academic study that might have loosely been related to the claims. *What questions would you need to ask about the study behind the headlines? What information do you want to know in order to decide how accurate the tweets, Facebook postings, blogs, and anecdotal stories are about the research?*

Reading the original study you would see that all the women in the sample (men were not part of the research) actually *gained* weight over a period of time, but "compared with nondrinkers, initially normal-weight women who consumed a light to moderate amount of alcohol gained less weight and had a lower risk of becoming overweight and/or obese during 12.9 years of follow-up" (Wang et al., 2010: 453). *In what ways does this conclusion differ from the headline's version of the research?*

Notice that the sensational headline does not indicate that this study (1) was at least five years old; (2) consisted of a women-only sample; (3) looked at self-reported alcohol consumption of all types, not just wine, and at any time, not just at bedtime; and (4) most important, did not in any way demonstrate that drinking wine caused weight loss. So much for "Wine as a Bedtime Snack Helps with Weight Loss," as a wine blog exclaimed (VinePair, 2015)!

Media reports of legitimate and scientific research often tell us what foods, diets, vitamins, and physical exercises are best for preventing illnesses and early death. To take one example, studies about the impact on our health of gluten in foods found evidence of sensitivity in people without celiac disease (an intestinal condition that is strongly controlled by gluten-free diets). However, a few years later, the same investigators in another scientific study concluded there was no specific response to a gluten diet among nonceliac gluten-sensitive people (Biesiekierski, Muir, and Gibson, 2013). Media reports of research like these studies often leave out important information about whom researchers sampled, how many participated in a study, and what valid and reliable research methods were used. *How do we begin to get a handle on all of these sometimes-contradictory studies and determine the quality of their research methodologies?*

Consider another kind of communication requiring critical thinking. Every year around the time for income-tax preparation, fake U.S. Internal Revenue Service (IRS) agents call people demanding back payments. It is estimated that thousands of people have fallen for the ruse and contributed over $20 million to these con artists. The IRS even warns that caller IDs are "spoofed" to look like they're coming from a government-agency telephone. Furthermore, unlike the IRS, scammers talk over the phone about you owing more money, ask for immediate payment especially with prepaid debit cards or wire transfer, and issue threats to vulnerable and ill-informed citizens about losing a job, house, or car. *What kinds of skills help you to decide whether such a communication is a scam or legitimate?*

Each day we are also confronted with distorted and inaccurate information from politicians, media advertisers, pollsters, cable news "experts," and friends passing along unfounded rumors. Websites during the 2016 U.S. presidential election sent out *fake news* reports, including that Pope Francis supported Donald Trump and that Hillary Clinton sold weapons to ISIS (Wingfield, Isaac, and Benner, 2016). With 44 percent of the general U.S. population getting their news from Facebook (Pew Research Center, 2016b), social media and search engines like Google have been pressured into controlling fake reports that appear in news feeds and searches.

An analysis of online news items in 2016 found that the "20 top-performing false election stories from hoax sites and hyperpartisan blogs generated 8,711,000 shares, reactions, and comments on Facebook. Within the same time period, the 20 best-performing election stories from 19 major news websites generated a total of 7,367,000 shares, reactions, and comments on Facebook" (Silverman, 2016). Websites like PolitiFact and Snopes were created to monitor the truthfulness of many public figures' proclamations, Internet rumors, and fake news scams. *What impact do you think social media play in making false stories go viral and impacting public policy like elections?*

Less benign are the urban legends that get "shared" on Facebook, "retweeted" through Twitter, and forwarded in emails. Although some of these posts are part of the social media game, and can be fun, many times scams following a disastrous flood or tornado, for example, take a psychological and financial toll on people and their families. *What steps do you need to take in order to evaluate the accuracy of rumors and media statements from public figures? What tools help you become critical thinkers?*

In a survey sponsored by the Association of American Colleges & Universities (AAC&U), 93 percent of nonprofit and business employers in the sample said that "a demonstrated capacity to think critically, communicate clearly, and solve complex problems is more important than [a candidate's] undergraduate major" (Hart Research Associates, 2013: 4). A survey of one thousand teachers by EdSource in partnership with the California Teachers Association also found that "when asked to rank the most important indicators of college and career readiness, 78 percent of teachers ranked developing critical thinking skills among the three most important indicators" (Freedberg, 2015). In addition, critical thinking has become a central component of common core standards in most American states' school curricula.

Educators, parents, and opinion leaders often bemoan the lack of critical thinking in our lives, in our media, and—perhaps most seriously—in our school programs. As Klinenberg (2016) wrote:

> There's one other thing that universities must do better: teach students skills for learning, discerning, reasoning, and communicating in an informational environment dominated by quick hits on social media like Twitter and Facebook. . . . Professors know how to help students work through difficult ideas in books and articles. But except for some of us in the learning sciences, few

of us have thought much about how to help students develop critical thinking skills for the media that they use most.

How do we teach these basic and essential skills of critical thinking? What does teaching involve? How effective is critical thinking? What does it actually mean? And how does critical thinking apply to evaluating the research we hear about in the media and read in academic and popular articles?

DEFINING CRITICAL THINKING

There are many approaches to the subject of critical thinking and different ways of defining it. Perhaps it's first important to explain what it is *not*. For some, the word "critical" may mean to find fault with or to judge unfairly. We think of critics as people who have to constantly complain about something and to impose their personal opinions. Others see critical thinking as a form of skepticism that can sometimes lead to cynicism, whereas gullibility is viewed as a result of a dearth of skepticism and critical thinking skills.

Shermer (1997) defines *skepticism* as a provisional approach and rational method to claims; it seeks evidence to prove or disprove the validity of these claims. One main tool of skepticism is the critical thinking embodied in scientific methodologies. A misguided skepticism, though, can result in a closing of the mind to potentially new ways of seeing things. Being totally closed off to different views and innovative thinking can make one easily fooled and tricked into believing something that is not true: that is, to being gullible. *Cynicism,* on the other hand, is defined as a distrust of people's motives based on a belief that self-interest and greed typically guide decision making and behavior. It is a pessimistic view that reveals a disparaging attitude to what people do and say, sometimes as a result of excessive skepticism. Critical thinking should involve finding the tools to develop a healthy skepticism without becoming too cynical or gullible. The noted astronomer Carl Sagan (1987) said it well:

> It seems to me what is called for is an exquisite balance between two conflicting needs: the most skeptical scrutiny of all hypotheses that are served up to us and at the same time a great openness to new ideas. Obviously those two modes of thought are in some tension. But if you are able to exercise only one of these modes, whichever one it is, you're in deep trouble. If you are only skeptical, then no new ideas make it through to you. You never learn anything new. . . . On the other hand, if you are open to the point of gullibility

and have not an ounce of skeptical sense in you, then you cannot distinguish the useful ideas from the worthless ones. If all ideas have equal validity then you are lost, because then, it seems to me, no ideas have any validity at all.

The emphasis in this book is the development of critical thinking skills that can ward off gullibility, improve analytical reasoning, develop insightful skepticism, and lead to interpreting and creating reliable and valid research methodologies. It's not a book providing you with information and data to disprove or support the arrival of UFOs, the existence of Bigfoot, or the health benefits of antioxidants in your food. Rather, the focus is on creating a methodology—a toolbox of analytical skills—for you to ask the right questions about the research and stories you hear or read about online, in the mass media, or in scholarly publications. The goal is to provide critical thinking methods for "the careful application of reason in the determination of whether a claim is true" (Moore and Parker, 2009: 3). *What critical thinking tools do you need to decide on the legitimacy of facts, the meaning of opinions, and the truthfulness of claims?*

Focusing on critical thinking is not a recent phenomenon. Its Western roots can be found in Socrates, who extolled rational thought, the search for evidence, an analysis of reasons and assumptions, and logical consistency. Plato, Aristotle, and the Greek Skeptics further developed this Socratic method of probing and questioning and emphasized the importance of systematic, well-reasoned thinking. In contemporary terms, critical thinking can emphasize the wording of questions, the sources of opinion and fact, and the method and quality of information collection (Paul, Elder, and Bartell, 1997). Almost 20 years ago, Diane Halpern (1998: 450) made the case for it in language that could have been written today:

> People now have an incredible wealth of information available, quite literally at their fingertips, via the Internet and other remote services with only a few minutes of search time on the computer. The problem has become knowing what to do with the deluge of data. The information has to be selected, interpreted, digested, evaluated, learned, and applied or it is of no more use on a computer screen than it is on a library shelf. . . . The dual abilities of knowing how to learn and knowing how to think clearly about the rapidly proliferating information that they will be required to deal with will provide education for citizens of the 21st century.

Let's use the following definitions as frameworks for this book's approach. For the AAC&U (Rhodes, 2010a), "Critical thinking is a habit of mind characterized by the comprehensive exploration of issues, ideas, artifacts, and events before accepting or formulating an opinion or conclusion." Ennis (2015) sees critical thinking as "reasonable reflective thinking focused on deciding what to believe or do." A critical thinker, he said,

1. is open-minded and mindful of alternatives;
2. desires to be, and is, well informed;
3. judges well the credibility of sources;
4. identifies reasons, assumptions, and conclusions;
5. asks appropriate clarifying questions;
6. judges well the quality of an argument, including its reasons, assumptions, and evidence, and their degree of support for the conclusion;
7. can well develop and defend a reasonable position regarding a belief or an action, doing justice to challenges;
8. formulates plausible hypotheses;
9. plans and conducts experiments well;
10. defines terms in a way appropriate for the context;
11. draws conclusions when warranted—but with caution;
12. integrates all the above aspects of critical thinking.

Translating these ideas into more specific and measurable outcomes becomes an important task for educators. With the support of the National Science Foundation, Tennessee Tech University, as an illustration, developed the Critical Thinking Assessment Test (CAT, 2016). Its goal is to assess the following four skills:

EVALUATING INFORMATION
- Separate factual information from inferences.
- Interpret numerical relationships in graphs.
- Understand the limitations of correlational data.
- Evaluate evidence and identify inappropriate conclusions.

CREATIVE THINKING
- Identify alternative interpretations for data or observations.
- Identify new information that may support or contradict a hypothesis.
- Explain how new information can change a problem.

LEARNING AND PROBLEM SOLVING

- Separate relevant from irrelevant information.
- Integrate information to solve problems.
- Learn and apply new information.
- Use mathematical skills to solve real-world problems.

COMMUNICATION

- Communicate ideas effectively.

Another way of understanding the concept of critical thinking is to reach back to the great Socratic method of questioning. Neil Postman and Charles Weingartner's classic *Teaching as a Subversive Activity* (1969) begins with a chapter creatively titled "Crap Detecting," which challenges teachers to avoid the "information dissemination" approach to learning. Instead, education should be preparing students to develop "the attitudes and skills of social, political, and cultural criticism" by using a Socratic style of inquiry. This method of pedagogy is based on questioning: "Once you have learned how to ask questions—relevant and appropriate and substantial questions—you have learned how to learn and no one can keep you from learning whatever you want or need to know" (Postman and Weingartner, 1969: 23).

Asking the best questions that can lead to informative insights about what is reported in the print and visual media, academic publications, and social media requires learning some basics of scientific research methods. *How do you learn to crap-detect what you read and hear in everyday life?*

Browne and Keeley (2007) argue that critical thinking involves a "panning for gold" approach rather than a "sponge" method of learning. Although it's important to absorb information and opinions like a sponge in order to build a foundation for critical thinking, it is a passive way of accumulating knowledge without any methodology to decide which material to accept or reject. A question-asking technique, on the other hand, is what Browne and Keeley (2007: 5) call "panning for gold," since it requires the reader to ask a number of questions through continuous interactions with the material with the intention "to critically evaluate the material and formulate personal conclusions based on the evaluation."

They offer these suggested questions to ask when actively engaging with claims, beliefs, and arguments (Browne and Keeley, 2007: 13):

1. What are the issues and the conclusions?
2. What are the reasons?
3. Which words or phrases are ambiguous?
4. What are the value conflicts and assumptions?
5. What are the descriptive assumptions?
6. Are there any fallacies in the reasoning?
7. How good is the evidence?
8. Are there rival causes?
9. Are the statistics deceptive?
10. What significant information is omitted?
11. What reasonable conclusions are possible?

These questions underlie the concepts and methods developed in this book: reviewing the statistics (numeracy, charts, visual images), suggesting rival alternative explanations (before causation is established), uncovering information that has been left out of media reports of research (sampling, wording of questionnaire items), establishing how good the evidence is (reliability, validity, scientific methods), and making reasonable conclusions (biased and ambiguous interpretations, opinions and values selectively applied).

As these definitions suggest, critical thinking is not just about passive learning; it's also about actively doing and learning how to learn. Developing skills to interpret information and clarify beliefs is one dimension. Another aspect is learning the most appropriate skills and valid methods to critically evaluate material, to accurately communicate knowledge and information, and to create valid and reliable new research.

FOCUS OF THE BOOK

The critical thinking skills described by these definitions provide guidance to the design of this book. Emphasis is on (a) understanding common errors in thinking, (b) identifying methods required to evaluate information and interpret results, (c) learning social science concepts needed to make sense of both popular and academic claims, and (d) communicating, applying, and integrating the methods learned.

Each chapter focuses on key methods and concepts central to developing critical thinking and includes:

- identifying and defining the concept, idea, error, or method;
- providing examples from both scholarly and popular publications illustrating the definition, concept, or method;
- making connections to other related critical thinking concepts or ideas;
- providing exercises, critical thinking tips, and questions for readers to engage with and apply the method or concept discussed.

While presenting ways to interpret and critically think about the research you read or hear about, this book also serves as a supplementary guide to a more detailed social science methodology textbook. Consider this a critical thinking toolbox providing ideas, skills, and questions to ask when encountering media reports, claims of facts, and academic methodologies.

Chapter 1. Numeracy

Assessing critical thinking includes how successfully you "use mathematical skills to solve real-world problems," to quote one of the Critical Thinking Assessment Test (CAT) skills. So it's important to know not just how to perform basic mathematical functions; it's also crucial to develop a sense of understanding, representing, using, and analyzing numbers. Learning to interpret data and making estimates of what may be reasonable about a set of numerical findings are important skills. Chapter 1 provides examples of how to analyze and reason about quantitative information by exploring types of variables, units of measurement, averages (mean vs. median), and other ways to discuss numbers. To think critically involves being able to demonstrate quantitative reasoning through the analysis and estimation of numbers.

Chapter 2. Sampling

Assessing critical thinking, as stated above, includes how well you "evaluate evidence and identify inappropriate conclusions." Generalizing from biased samples, making inferences about groups of people not actually surveyed, and misunderstanding sampling methods commonly lead to problematic conclusions and interpretations. Faced with numerous surveys and polls as well as constant advertisements pushing anecdotal evidence, critical readers need to understand the basics of sampling methods and how to interpret findings when different samples are surveyed. This chapter presents information about various sampling techniques and highlights what it really means to have a "random" sample, a phrase often misused in everyday speech. Illustrations from good and inadequate samples in the popular media and published research provide ways to critically think about the sample rather than jump to inappropriate conclusions.

Chapter 3. Probability and Coincidence

Analyzing numerical information and sampling strategies also involves understanding probabilities. This chapter presents some aspects of probability theory and how best to think critically about odds when making decisions. Not only do we need to understand what it means to conclude statistical significance when conducting and reading research; we also require probability skills to reasonably evaluate risks confronted in everyday situations and as presented in the media or through rumors. Distinguishing between coincidences and probable outcomes is an important component of critical thinking.

Chapter 4. Visual Thinking

Assessing critical thinking includes the ability to "interpret numerical relationships in graphs." This chapter presents ways to recognize faulty and misleading graphs and charts while providing skills to accurately communicate information and to correctly interpret tables of data. Note how often visualizations can enhance information and how often they can confuse and mislead. Analyzing accurately the nonverbal elements of online media, corporate or financial information, and scholarly studies is an essential tool of critical thinking.

Chapter 5. Correlation and Causation

"Understand the limitations of correlational data" is a stated goal of the Critical Thinking Assessment Test (CAT, 2016) and other critical thinking evaluation measures. Chapter 5 focuses on a common error when people jump from meaningful correlations to conclusions of causality. Ruling out plausible alternative explanations and determining a timeline of occurrence between one variable and others are necessary steps before declaring a cause-and-effect finding. This chapter also illustrates a creative thinking skill stated earlier: "Identify alternative interpretations for data or observations." Learning about the use of explanatory variables that may be suppressing a real finding, that could intervene between two variables seemingly related, or that can explain away a seemingly causal relationship is explored in this chapter.

Chapter 6. Scientific Thinking

"Formulating plausible hypotheses" and learning to "identify new information that may support or contradict a hypothesis" are skills mentioned in several definitions and assessments of critical thinking (CAT, 2016). This chapter investigates what science is and how it is distinguished from pseudoscience. At the center are scientific methodology and systematic procedures that involve testing hypotheses, using control group designs to compare findings, applying probability statistics to measure chance occurrences, and the role of placebos in double-blind studies. Additional research designs are explored, such as Big Data, prospective epidemiological studies, and meta-analysis.

Chapter 7. Fact, Opinion, and Logical Reasoning

Assessing critical thinking includes the ability, as noted above, to "separate factual information from inferences" and to "separate relevant from irrelevant information." Too often, we confuse fact with opinion, and present conclusions—sometimes even based on actual data—that are not logically connected to the findings. Learning to "evaluate evidence and identify inappropriate conclusions," as indicated earlier, is a critical thinking skill. The power to deduce, make inferences, and uncover the logic when reading data, academic studies, and popular online media is important, and it is essential when communicating ideas effectively. This chapter pulls together the key ideas of the book by drawing on how facts, opinion, logic, and reasoning are central to a scientific and critical thinking methodology.

CRITICAL THINKING OBJECTIVE

When you have completed reading this book, your tool kit of critical thinking methods and skills will have been enhanced. It is just a beginning, though, to passively read about them. Critical thinking also requires practicing with these tools. It is not only a state of mind and a method for analyzing information and claims; critical thinking is an activity that requires performing and doing. With that in mind, here is the first of many Critical Thinking Tips scattered throughout the chapters to help you act on what you are learning.

CRITICAL THINKING TIP

Apply what you learn from the book! Even though numerous academic studies and popular media reports illustrate the key ideas throughout the text, keep in mind that no one study is perfect. Each has its limitations, caveats about its methods, and problems with its research design. Using them to provide examples for the concepts and methods introduced in each chapter does not mean that they are free of these limitations. It would take another entire book to review every aspect of each study or report quoted. You are encouraged to apply your critical thinking skills by reviewing the REFERENCES listed at the end of the book and using them to read the original research articles, to go to the online links, and to evaluate the media reports firsthand. In addition, try the EXERCISES at the end of each chapter; answer the Socratic-like QUESTIONS in italics embedded throughout the text—or at least pause for a moment to think about the issue; reflect on the "Critical Thinking Tips" presented in the chapters' BOXES; and go to the website designed for this book.

Given how many research findings and distorted reports appear daily in this social-mediated world, this website provides additional, updated examples, references, and further readings. As you read each chapter, visit the website to see current ideas, review articles referenced in the book, and participate in an online discussion: **https://criticalthinkingtext .wordpress.com/**.

CHAPTER 1

Numeracy

Critical Thinking, Step One: What do the numbers and statistics tell you? When hearing or reading about research results, often the first things you notice are the data. Perhaps the initial step in critically thinking about any claims made is to understand the data and how accurate the numbers, averages, and percentages are. Learning to interpret data, read statistics, and make estimates of what may be reasonable about a set of numerical findings is a good place to begin. Understanding, representing, using, and analyzing numbers are important tools of critical thinking and numeracy.

When asked, most people claim they are better drivers or fairer or smarter than the average person. It is not atypical for people to overestimate their abilities: As Zuckerman and Jost state (2001: 209): "Desires for self-enhancement and positive self-presentation lead people to make self-serving comparisons between themselves and others. Thus most people believe that they are 'better than average' on a wide variety of traits, abilities, and outcomes." How is it possible for most of us all to be better than average? What makes this statement suspicious depends on knowing something about percentages, averages, and their mathematical properties. More important, it requires overcoming a block some people have when dealing with numbers—what has been termed "innumeracy" (Paulos, 1989).

Learning to interpret data and make estimates of what may be reasonable about a set of quantitative findings is essential to thinking critically. Just knowing how to perform basic mathematical functions is not the important thing; it's also crucial to develop a sense of understanding, representing, using, and analyzing numbers. Deciphering and interpreting numbers with confidence are central elements of "numeracy," "quantitative reasoning," or "mathematical literacy." *Numeracy* is a building block of critical thinking. The California Critical Thinking Skills Test-Numeracy (2016) defines it as the ability to solve quantitative reasoning problems and to make well-reasoned judgments derived from quantitative information in a variety of contexts. More than being able to compute or calculate a solution to a mathematical equation, numeracy includes understanding how quantitative information is gathered, represented, and correctly interpreted using graphs, charts, tables and diagrams.

According to the Association of American Colleges & Universities (Rhodes, 2010b), *quantitative literacy* involves:

- *interpretation* (ability to explain information presented in mathematical forms—e.g., equations, graphs, diagrams, tables, words),
- *representation* (ability to convert relevant information into various mathematical forms—e.g., equations, graphs, diagrams, tables, words),
- *calculation* (successful and sufficiently comprehensive to solve the problem clearly),
- *application/analysis* (ability to make judgments and draw appropriate conclusions based on the quantitative analysis of data while recognizing the limits of this analysis),
- *assumptions* (ability to make and evaluate important assumptions in estimation, modeling, and data analysis), and
- *communication* (expressing quantitative evidence in support of the argument or purpose of the work).

An element of quantitative reasoning is developing confidence with statistics. The American Statistical Association (GAISE, 2015: 11–12) wants students to believe and understand why:

- data beat anecdotes;
- variability is natural, predictable, and quantifiable;
- random sampling allows results of surveys and experiments to be extended to the population from which the sample was taken;
- random assignment in comparative experiments allows cause-and-effect conclusions to be drawn;
- association is not causation;
- statistical significance does not necessarily imply practical importance, especially for studies with large sample sizes;

- finding no statistically significant difference or relationship does not necessarily mean there is no difference or relationship in the population, especially for studies with small sample sizes.

In addition (GAISE, 2015: 12), students should recognize:

- common sources of bias in surveys and experiments;
- how to determine the population to which the results of statistical inference can be extended, if any, based on how the data were collected;
- how to determine when a cause-and-effect inference can be drawn from an association based on how the data were collected (e.g., the design of the study);
- that words such as "normal," "random," and "correlation" have specific meanings in statistics that may differ from common usage.

These quantitative-reasoning and numeracy goals and skills are addressed in this chapter and subsequent ones, with the emphasis less on calculation and more on learning the basic tools required to interpret, represent, critically analyze, and communicate quantitatively.

Let's consider below several basic concepts relevant to developing a critical ability to evaluate common everyday reports that use or misuse numbers: percentages, margin of error, levels of measurement, central tendency measures (averages), and estimations.

PERCENTAGES

In the summer of 2015, the California Highway Patrol (CHP) "released a new study showing a 39 percent increase in the percentage of California drivers seen using a cell phone while driving." That figure is based on 9.2 percent of drivers on a cell phone in 2015 compared with 6.6 percent in 2014. CHP also said "law enforcement wrote 35 percent more tickets for texting-while-driving compared to 2014" (California Highway Patrol, 2015).

The short press release received much attention in the media. Details about the study, however, were not in the brief announcement, thus illustrating a problematic way of reporting the results of research. To find out the relevant details left out of the announcement or news broadcast, you had to make an effort to go online to read the complete report. *What more information would you want in order to make sense out of this too-brief media report of survey findings? How do you decide whether these 39 percent, 9.2 percent, and 6.6 percent figures are meaningful or not?*

In the CHP study (Ewald and Waserman Research Consultants, 2015), we are told that the researchers saw 9.2 percent of drivers on a cell phone in 2015. The first question to ask is, How many drivers were studied? We need to know the denominator. Remember, a percentage is a proportion calculated by dividing a subset of items (numerator) by the total number of items (denominator) and then multiplied by 100 (*per centum* is Latin meaning "per one hundred"). Sometimes you will read findings "per capita" (Latin for "per head": that is, per person) and "per 1,000" as the World Bank (2014) does in reporting the number of physicians for every 1,000 people in countries around the world (such as Australia, 3.3; Canada, 2.1; Kenya, 0.2). Sometimes you may even see "per 10,000" which the World Health Organization (2013: 122, 125) uses in reporting the number of hospital beds globally (like Ethiopia, 63; New Zealand, 23). These kinds of standardization (percent, per 1,000, etc.) allow us to compare findings among samples of different sizes.

Consider how important this ability to standardize is when deciding whether to report data in terms of absolute numbers as opposed to percentages. For example, it would be accurate to report that Californians hold the most passports among all Americans, averaging close to 2.5 million per year. As the most populous state, with nearly 40 million residents, this shouldn't be a surprising finding. But using raw numbers when comparing states of different populations distorts the message. It turns out that California is actually behind six other states, including less populous states like Alaska and Delaware, when taking into account the relative population of the states: that is, when calculating the percentage of citizens with passports (Stabile, 2016).

CRITICAL THINKING TIP

When comparing numbers taken from samples or populations of different sizes, be sure to report both the absolute numbers and the percentages (per 100 or per 1,000 or per capita) so that comparisons can be made. Be critical when only raw numbers are presented, without the total number in each of the comparison groups being provided.

Understanding how to read or calculate an accurate percentage is one step in learning numeracy and thinking critically. It's also important to understand what is meant when reports discuss a percentage increase or decrease over time. Recall the CHP cell-phone-use-while-driving study: 9.2 percent of drivers on a cell phone is 39 percent higher than the previous year's 6.6 percent. *How can 9.2 be 39 percent higher than 6.6?*

At the simplest level, a percentage point increase or decrease is a difference between two percentages, so you could say that cell phone usage went up 2.6 percent in one year (9.2 minus 6.6 equals 2.6 percentage point increase). Some may erroneously misinterpret the "39 percent higher" to mean that driving while on a cell phone increased from 6.6 percent to 45.6 percent. This isn't the case, yet it's easy to see how some misunderstanding or distorted findings can be communicated when not critically asking what the numbers represent.

To arrive at the 39 percent increase, you take the percentage point difference and then divide it by the original percentage (2.6/6.6) to get 0.394 or 39.4 percent (multiply by 100 to get a percentage). Note that the percentage point difference is 2.6, and the percentage increase over time is 39.4. The fact that those are two different numbers can create confusion in readers of data, and can sometimes purposely be used unethically to inflate or deflate actual change.

For example, imagine a shift from 20 percent of a sample in an election political poll supporting Candidate A to 30 percent a few months later. This ten percentage point increase indicates a modest shift in support for the struggling politician, who still does not have a majority. Simply take the percentage point difference and divide it by the original percentage (10/20 = 0.50). Yet, it would be easy to distort the findings to suggest a surge of interest in the candidate by reporting a "tremendous 50 percent improvement" in popularity. Although the statement would be accurate, those without numeracy skills might mistakenly think the candidate went up 50 points in the polls, from 20 percent to 70 percent, focusing on the number 50 rather than the much smaller 30.

Look at this paragraph from a *New York Times* article (Saulny, 2011) about an increase in multiracial people in the 2010 U.S. Census: "In North Carolina, the mixed-race population doubled. In Georgia, it expanded by more than 80 percent, and by nearly as much in Kentucky and Tennessee. In Indiana, Iowa and South Dakota, the multiracial population increased by about 70 percent." Note the word "doubled" and the large numbers, 80 and 70. Sounds impressive. A few paragraphs later the article reports a possible national multiracial growth rate of 35 percent, maybe even a 50 percent increase from the last census, in 2000. Again, these are large and impressive numbers. *What kinds of missing information do you need to better understand these percentages?*

Then the article states that in 2000 only 2.4 percent of Americans selected more than one race on the census form. It's one thing to claim that the multiracial population may increase 50 percent, but when the original figure is only 2.4 percent of Americans, a 50 percent increase simply means that the 2010 multiracial population could end up around 3.6 percent of the population. (50% of 2.4 = 1.2, and 2.4 + 1.2 = 3.6.) The number 50 surely sounds more impressive than the smaller figure, 3.6. Manipulating these numbers can create misleading impressions, sometimes unethically done with intention.

By the way, in the 2010 United States Census, 2.9 percent identified as two or more races, while the Pew Research Center (2015a) estimates that 6.9 percent of the U.S. population could be considered multiracial when including "how adults describe their own race as well as the racial backgrounds of their parents and grandparents." Understanding how researchers calculated the number and how it was measured are important questions to ask when interpreting data. *Which percentage makes more sense to you, 2.9 or 6.9? What questions would you ask to determine if respondents are multiracial?*

Being able to interpret numbers correctly often comes down to reporting all the relevant data. In the *New York Times* article, we really do not have enough information to know exactly what the multiracial population is in the states listed. That they doubled in North Carolina and increased 80 percent in Georgia tells us little about the actual 2000 or 2010 census figures in those states.

CRITICAL THINKING TIP

Always identify clearly the items being compared (when, where, and what) and express differences as percentages of the initial reference values. (See Miller, 2004.) After all, an increase of 75 cents when purchasing a cappuccino is more annoying (and a much higher percentage change) than the same amount tacked on to the price of a new car!

MARGIN OF ERROR

When political polls show that Candidate A has 46 percent of the popular vote and Candidate B has 42 percent, we cannot conclude that Candidate A is winning, despite announcements that A is ahead. Before making this statement, critical thinkers need to ask what the *margin of error* for the poll is. If the margin of error is plus or minus 4 percent, then it would suggest that Candidate A has between 42 percent and 50 percent support in the total population from which the sample was selected, and Candidate B has between 38 percent and 46 percent. There is a lot of overlap in support, and it could well be that A's true support percentage is, for example, 43 percent, whereas B's is 46 percent. Both those figures are within each candidate's margin of error.

The margin of error is based on sampling issues (see chapter 2) assuming that randomly selected respondents reflect the characteristics of a population with some, but not perfect, accuracy. Usually, the margin of error specifies how confident the researcher is in generalizing a statistical finding to the total population based on a random sample of a particular size drawn from that population. Here is the Pew Research Center's (2016a) statement about their survey practices:

> The sampling error for a typical Pew Research Center national survey of 1,500 completed interviews is plus or minus approximately 3 percentage points with a 95% confidence interval. This means that in 95 out of every 100 samples of the same size and type, the results we would obtain will vary by no more than plus or minus 3 percentage points from the result we would get if we could interview every member of the population. Thus, the chances are very high (95 out of 100) that any sample we draw will be within 3 points of the true population value.

CRITICAL THINKING TIP

When reading political polls or results from a survey, be sure to look for the margin of error. Then add and subtract that number from the results presented. Only then will you be able to critically analyze the findings and understand the range of possible results.

Consider the margin of error in Pew Research Center's (2015b) study about teenagers' friendships and romantic relationships in the digital age. As table 1 indicates, any results from the parents surveyed should

TABLE I   MARGINS OF ERROR

Category	Sample size	Margin of error (percentage points)
All parents	1,060	±3.4
All teens	1,060	±3.7
Girls	537	±5.2
Boys	523	±5.3
White, non-Hispanic	614	±4.5
Black, non-Hispanic	101	±13.3
Hispanic	236	±8.1
Teen cellphone owners	929	±3.9
Teen smartphone owners	759	±4.4
Teen social media users	789	±4.3

SOURCE: Pew Research Center (2015b).

NOTE: These margins of error are based on the individual sizes of each subsample category and are used to interpret each subsample's answers to the survey questions (not reported here).

be viewed as accurate 95 percent of the time within plus or minus 3.4 percentage points of the figure reported. Notice how size of sample impacts the margin of error: With only 101 black teenagers surveyed, any responses to individual survey questions should be interpreted as being within plus or minus 13.3 percentage points of the reported result.

In the survey, 79 percent of all teens said that they instant-messaged their friends. With the margin of error for all teens at 3.7 percent, this means that if Pew were to complete 100 surveys with a similar random sample of 1,060 teens, 95 of the surveys would report a finding between 75.3 percent and 82.7 percent of teens texting their friends (79 − 3.7 and 79 + 3.7). That is, there is a high probability (95%) that the Pew Research Center sample finding of 79 percent is within plus or minus 3.7 percent of the true value in the total population.

Here's a situation where margin of error resulted in some arbitrary decisions with important political ramifications. For the Fox News Channel's (FNC's) first Republican Party U.S. presidential candidates' debate, in August 2015, FNC decided to use an average of several polls to determine the ten most popular participants. What's evident in table 2 is that the margins of error for each candidate in the average of five opinion polls made deciding who should be in and who should be out a difficult choice among those in the tenth through fourteenth positions (Kurtzleben, 2015). *How would you interpret these findings using the concept of the margin of error?*

TABLE 2   POLL DATA USED TO DETERMINE REPUBLICAN-PARTY PRESIDENTIAL-NOMINEE DEBATE PARTICIPANTS, 2015–16

Candidate	Average percent[a]	Margin of error (percentage points)
Donald Trump	23.4	±2.19
Jeb Bush	12.0	±1.66
Scott Walker	10.2	±1.51
Marco Rubio	5.4	±0.70
Rand Paul	4.8	±0.66
Mike Huckabee	6.6	±0.70
Ben Carson	5.8	±0.66
Ted Cruz	5.4	±0.70
Chris Christie	3.4	±0.43
John Kasich	3.2	±1.16
Rick Perry	1.8	±0.35
Bobby Jindal	1.4	±0.43
Rick Santorum	1.4	±0.43
Carly Fiorina	1.2	±0.66

SOURCE: Based on Kurtzleben, 2015.

[a]Average percent from multiple polls indicating voters' preferences for the Republican presidential nomination.

LEVELS OF MEASUREMENT

Calculating percentages and margins of error, however, depends on the level of measurement used in a study. *Level of measurement* refers to the type of values that characterize the elements of a variable. For example, imagine a survey asking, "What type of music do you listen to?" In this case, "music type" is a *variable* (a concept that varies); "folk," "rap," "classical," and "show tunes" could be the *values* used to measure that variable. The method used to determine the values is called the level of measurement.

Consider for a moment the *Billboard* Top 200 music chart. *How do you create a list of the top best-selling music when the concept of an album has changed?* For years, the Top 200 entailed counting sales of physical vinyl records and CDs by scanning bar codes. Then along came purchasing digital music online (such as from iTunes and Amazon Prime) and streaming music (such as with Spotify and Pandora). *Billboard* (2014), based on Nielsen Entertainment's measurements, counts "10 digital track sales from an album to one equivalent album sale, and 1,500 song streams from an album to one equivalent album sale."

Why not 1,600 streams or nine digital tracks? As you can see, writing a question for a survey and measuring the answer is not necessarily a simple or objective process. Assessing how questions are posed and how concepts are measured are essential steps in critical thinking and very important in determining which levels of measurement to select.

Look back at how percentages and margins of error are calculated. The numbers must be such that they can be added, subtracted, divided, and multiplied. These basic mathematical operations cannot be performed on numerals, figures that look like numbers but really aren't. *When is a number not a number?*

Imagine a survey asking the following question:

What is your favorite type of movie?

1. Foreign language
2. Animation
3. Drama
4. Comedy

Note that a discrete number has been assigned to each answer category. Just as easily, 1 could have been assigned to animation, or 3 to comedy. That's because the numbers here are actually arbitrary numerals, with no intrinsic order (is drama "higher than" animation?) and no intensity (is comedy twice as meaningful as animation?). Letters could also have been selected, (a) Foreign Language; (b) Animation, and so forth. In such cases, we refer to this type of level of measurement as *Nominal* or *Categorical*. Any numbers assigned to the categories (values of a variable) are simply numerals, without any mathematical properties.

CRITICAL THINKING TIP

Do a quick, basic mathematical operation on the numbers you are reading to see if they make sense. Take your friends' phone numbers and add, subtract, multiply, and divide them. What do you get? Is there an average phone number? Maybe they're not numbers but numerals after all, and we should really ask for someone's "phone numeral" instead!

Sometimes the categories are in order, such as shirt sizes: 1, small; 2, medium; 3, large; 4, extra large. You could call 1 extra large; 2, large;

3, medium; 4, small; but you certainly cannot assign numbers this way: 1, medium; 2, small; 3, extra large; 4, large. Once the categories have been ordered, any discrete numeral must also be assigned in order from low to high or high to low. Hence, these are called *ordinal* measures. Yet, these numerals do not have any mathematical properties allowing them to be added, subtracted, multiplied, or divided. A small-sized shirt is not 25 percent (1/4 = 0.25) the size of an extra large one just because small is designated 1 and extra large is numbered 4. It is possible to have ordered numerals with equal-appearing intervals, called *Likert-type scales*, where 1 indicates strongly agree; 2, agree; 3, disagree; and 4, strongly disagree. Occasionally, these can be used as if they were actual numbers. (See the next section, on measurements of central tendency.)

Let's now consider measurements that have mathematical properties. In these cases, the numbers not only represent order but assume equal intervals between them. Some numbers are discrete (such as the number of books in a library, children in a family, or students enrolled in a class—with no fractions or numbers between the counting units), and others are continuous (like time, length, temperature, or age). These types of measurements are called *interval* or *ratio* measures. If there is an absolute zero—that is, no negative numbers, like age or weight—then you can calculate a ratio using multiplication and division. Given their mostly similar properties, these two measures are often labeled singly as *interval/ratio*.

CRITICAL THINKING TIP

Knowing the level of measurement is important when critically evaluating the correct use of graphs and charts, interpreting averages, and deciding whether appropriate statistics are being used. Ask how the variables in a report and questions in a survey are measured, and then decide whether the relevant statistics or charts are being employed.

CENTRAL TENDENCY MEASURES (AVERAGES)

Media reports often present survey results and other data in summary form. One common way is using averages, or more technically, *measures of central tendency*. Critically interpreting these measures requires evaluating what they are telling us about the summarized data and assessing whether the report is employing the best possible measure.

The media reported these numbers from the United States Census (2015):

Mean travel time to work (minutes), workers age 16+	25.7
Persons per household	2.63
Median household income	$53,482
Modal grade for 15-year-olds	10th grade

Where do we begin in understanding what is being reported? The first step in critically thinking about averages is to understand how a particular item is being measured. "Travel time" is the number of minutes it takes workers over the age of sixteen to get to work. Time is usually measured as a continuous-ratio variable, so mathematical operations can be performed, like adding them up and dividing by the total number to arrive at a calculation summary called the *mean*. All the people in the United States Census who completed that question about travel time gave a figure in minutes; these figures were summed and then divided by the number of people who answered the question. In popular jargon, when people refer to an average, it's usually this mathematical mean, as for example a GPA (grade-point average).

But take a look at the second reported average: 2.63 persons per U.S. household. Again, people responding to this question gave numbers that were all added together and then divided by the total number of respondents. Did some people say they were living with 0.63 of a person? *How can that be?* Well, the mathematical calculations on discrete interval/ratio numbers often end up with fractions of a person. Although a mean is correctly applied to interval/ratio data, when the numbers are not continuous, the resulting mean can sound pretty silly. The *World Factbook* (2015), for example, presents Total Fertility Rates (number of children born per woman) that sound peculiar, such as Afghanistan (5.33), Belgium (1.78), Canada (1.59), and Zimbabwe (3.53).

Related to the mathematical mean is an important concept called the *standard deviation*. Just knowing what the average is doesn't tell you much about what was measured. For example, someone may have a 3.0 (B) grade-point average because all her grades were B's. Yet, someone else could have a 3.0 (B) average with half his grades A and half C.

The mean does not tell the entire story. What is needed is a sense of the distribution of values that lead to a particular mathematical calculation.

A critical thinker is not satisfied simply with knowing the mean but inquires about the range of values obtained by a study. A standard deviation provides a more comprehensive description of what is found. A standard deviation of zero indicates that all the scores were the same; there was no variation from the mean. The student with a 3.0 GPA who had all B grades would have a standard deviation of zero. The larger the standard deviation, the more the scores are spread out (deviate) around the mean.

In some ways, the standard deviation is conceptually similar to the margin of error, in that it tells you what the probability is of finding a value close to or further away from the average. Recall how a margin of error indicates what range of values contains the true finding 95 percent of the time. Similarly, 95 percent of all values in a normal (bell-shaped) curve distribution are within two standard deviations below and above the mean. For example, consider a local high school's reading-comprehension test scores that are normally distributed with a mean score of 80 and a standard deviation of 7. Since it's greater than zero, we know that not all the students scored exactly 80, and so the grades must vary among the test takers. Based on the concept of the normal distribution, 95 percent of the students scored within two standard deviations above (7 + 7 = 14) and two standard deviations below the mean (−14), that is, between 94 (80 + 14) and 66 (80 − 14). Around 68 percent of them scored within one standard deviation above and below the mean. *What would be that range of scores?*

Sometimes an average can be a *median,* which is more appropriate for ordinal-level data or when there are extreme numbers (outliers) in the set of interval/ratio responses. The median (like the strip of land dividing a highway in half) is the point around which half the responses are higher and half are lower (the 50th percentile). Income is usually a good example, where the median is more relevant than the mathematical mean, as in the earlier United States Census example, since extreme incomes can distort the calculation and skew it in the direction of the few outlier scores.

Imagine you are calculating the mean age for kids hanging out in the local playground. To keep it small, let's say there are four kids, aged 1, 3, 4, and 6. The age of 3.5 would be the mathematical mean, and 3.5 would be the median point (halfway between 3 and 4) around which half the kids are older (the 4- and 6-year-olds) and half are younger than 3.5 (the two kids aged 1 and 3). Then all of a sudden a 16-year-old arrives in the park. The mean age now almost doubles, becoming 6 whereas the median increases incrementally to 4. When extreme scores appear in a set of data, the summary measure of central tendency should be the median. After all, if Mark Zuckerberg walked into a bar, everyone there would be a millionaire on average!

> **CRITICAL THINKING TIP**
>
> Whenever you read or hear about "an average," or something is "on average," first ask which kind of average is being used: mathematical mean, median, or mode. Then figure out how the item was measured (nominal, ordinal, interval/ratio) in order to make sure that the appropriate average has been selected. This is especially the case when there are extreme values, which require a median rather than a mean.

Take this example from the Pew Research Center's (2014) Internet Project survey: "Among adult Facebook users, the average (mean) number of friends is 338, and the median (midpoint) number of friends is 200." With the mean being much higher than the median, this suggests that among 960 Internet users sampled for the study, there are some people with much larger numbers of friends than the rest. The median is typically the best measure of central tendency to use when you have extreme numbers (either very high or very low) reported by some respondents. Note also how Pew correctly labeled the central tendency measures reported in their survey.

Finally, what to do with nominal data that have no order or numerical properties? At best, you can report only the most typical answer, called the *mode;* it's the response given in the greatest number of answers, though not always in the majority of them. The most common age for 10th graders is 15, as the census stated. Remember, a majority requires over 50 percent; and if one choice is over 50 percent, then it's certainly also the mode. But if one response is the one most often selected and it's under 50 percent, it's still the modal response even if not the majority answer. Modes can be used for nominal, ordinal, or interval/ratio data.

Using data from a General Social Survey (that asked its almost 2,500 respondents in 2014 how old they were, an interval/ratio measure), we find the mean was 49; median, 48; mode, 53, 56, and 58. These numbers tell us that the mathematical average age is 49, that half the sample is under 48 and half is over 48, and that the most common ages in the sample are 53, 56, 58. Those three ages each account for only 2.4 percent of the total, so clearly the finding is that none of those ages is the majority, only that this sample has multimodal ages (sometimes called bimodal—when there are only two modes).

ESTIMATIONS

During the 2016 U.S. presidential election, Donald Trump claimed Hillary Clinton wanted to let "650 million people pour" into the United States, thereby "tripling the size of our country in one week" (Valverde, 2016). *How realistic is this estimate of many millions of people entering a country in one week?* In 2014, survey respondents in Great Britain estimated that Muslims made up 21 percent of the U.K. population; Canadians thought that immigrants were 35 percent of their population; and Americans believed that 24 percent of girls between 15 and 19 years of age gave birth each year to a child (Nardelli and Arnett, 2014). Does it sound reasonable that so many teenaged girls give birth each year or that Canada had so many immigrants? Critical thinking requires you ask when hearing such claims: *How well do people know the real percentages when filling out a survey? How many of these numbers reflect actual percentages in those countries? How well can you make estimates and roughly judge the accuracy of the data?*

Learning to decipher the accuracy of numbers presented in studies and in the media is an important critical tool. One way, of course, is to get informed by seeking out original studies and relevant data to check claims made. Without immediate access to such information, however, a key numeracy and quantitative literacy skill is the ability to estimate and quickly recognize how close or off any reported number is. When reading survey results or hearing media reports filled with numbers and statistics, we should be able to estimate what a reasonable answer is before interpreting the findings and the accuracy of the reported figures.

Estimation is a close guess, often using some calculation or critical appraisal of the final value. As Steen and the Quantitative Literacy Design Team wrote (2001: 8): "Individuals who are quantitatively confident routinely use mental estimates to quantify, interpret, and check other information." We already make estimates in our everyday routines that are rough approximations of the actual outcome: How long it will take to drive to work at a given hour of the day; how much wrapping paper you need from the roll to fit around the birthday present you bought; or how many feet away you have to be to sink that ball in the basket. Estimating is a skill that improves with practice. It requires some knowledge of a standard or average number, often based on prior experience, in order to come up with some educated guess.

CRITICAL THINKING TIP

Ask yourself if the numbers that you are hearing or reading about are within a range you may expect. What would be your estimate for the results? If you're not sure, then inquire about where the data come from, what is being measured, who is calculating the findings, and how the researchers arrived at those figures.

Rounding off is a particularly useful trick when making estimates with numbers. If you were asked to figure out how many cups of coffee to have available for the reception following a speech by a well-known author, you would begin by estimating the number of people who could fill the auditorium. Say there are *about* 12 rows with *around* 14 seats in each, so in your head, round off to 10 rows by 15 seats for a quick estimate of at least 150 spaces. The actual number is 168, but 150 is close enough for a simple, quick estimate. If someone were to say that there would be room for 200 or 300 people sitting in on the lecture, you would immediately know that this is an overestimate.

Another method useful to estimating outcomes is comparing findings proportionately to their occurrence in a population. In the 2016 U.S. presidential election, about 50 percent of eligible citizens 18 to 29 years old voted. How do we estimate if this figure is high, low, or average? First we need to know what the overall voter turnout was for eligible voters. For that election, 58 percent of citizens voted. Without doing any statistical analysis, it looks like young adults voted at lower rates than the total population.

Another way of interpreting the percentage is to ask what proportion of the population is in that age range and evaluate whether the percentage of citizens 18–29 years old voting in 2016 is representative of that share of the population. Here we find that people 18–29 years old are around 17 percent of the U.S. citizen population, yet they make up about 19 percent of the votes cast (CNN, 2016). *What would you conclude from these different ways of reporting exit poll findings?*

From a math blog in England (Ellie's Active Maths, 2011):

> One of the best things about estimating is that we use our mathematical reasoning. There are often several ways to come to an answer, none of which is wrong. When a student comes up with an answer, we can ask them to explain, in words, their thought-process/reasoning. It encourages problem solving. Importantly, estimating allows us to check to see if our calculated answers are reasonable.

So it is with media stories and research studies: Estimating allows us to check to see if the information we are reading or hearing is reasonable. Is it really possible to have a city or school brag that all the children score above average on an intelligence test, now that you know that if it is a median average, half are above and half are below average? Is it reasonable to believe that one out of every four teenage girls in the United States gave birth to babies? (It's actually closer to 3 percent.) Could a little over a third of the Canadian population be immigrants? (It's actually around 20 percent.)

As we encounter various media reports, published survey findings, fake news sites, and politicians' pronouncements using numbers and other data, numeracy becomes a necessary tool in assessing the figures and measurements used. Learn to understand different kinds of measurements and averages. That's step one in critical thinking: interpreting what was found. We also need to assess who was studied and how by evaluating the methods that generated the sample, as chapter 2 shows.

KEY TERMS

ESTIMATIONS Close guesses, based on some rough calculation or by critically thinking what the findings should be.

INTERVAL/RATIO MEASURES Values of a variable in order with equal intervals and actual numbers that can be added, subtracted, multiplied, and divided.

LEVEL OF MEASUREMENT The type of value that characterizes the elements of a variable, such as nominal, ordinal, interval, and ratio.

MARGIN OF ERROR The differences between the true population statistic and the statistic found in a sample from that population, often specified in polls as plus or minus a percentage.

MEAN The mathematical measure of central tendency based on adding the values and dividing by the number of values.

MEDIAN A measure of central tendency that represents the halfway point among a range of ordered numbers.

MODE A measure of central tendency indicating the most frequently occurring value of a variable.

NOMINAL MEASURES Values of a variable using categories or numerals.

NUMERACY A critical thinking tool based on understanding, using, and evaluating numbers with confidence; quantitative literacy.

ORDINAL MEASURES Values of a variable that are in rank order.

PERCENTAGE A mathematical calculation that multiples a ratio by 100.

STANDARD DEVIATION An indication of the dispersion of values around a mathematical mean.

EXERCISES

1. An article on young-adult novels stated: "Thank J.K. Rowling for starting the kid's-book craze with 'Harry Potter' and Stephenie Meyer's 'Twilight' saga for perpetuating the trend that has more adults reading children's titles than ever before. The year 2011 has seen an explosion of books catering to this ever-expanding bimodal audience." (Carpenter, 2011). The typical reader might continue with the article and not raise any questions at this point. But as a *critical thinker,* you would want to raise and answer these questions: What is meant by the phrase "bimodal audience" and how do you think the author arrived at this statement? What data would you need to see? How would you go about conducting a survey to test out this idea; what kinds of questions would you ask to get different kinds of measurements besides the mode?

2. During a political campaign, one candidate tweeted excitedly to her followers that her polling numbers went up from 1 percent to 6 percent in three months. But it's less impressive when you consider that the *margin of error* for the latest poll is 4.7 percent (and was 5.3 percent for the first poll). Explain why the candidate needs to be more cautious about celebrating her poll numbers.

3. The media reports that the *average* American reads 12 books a year. When you first hear or read that headline, as a critical thinker, what questions do you need to ask? Then you see table 3, taken from a Pew Research Center report (2015c). Put into words what it's communicating to us about book reading in the United States.

TABLE 3 AVERAGE (MEAN) AMERICAN READERSHIP OVER
THE TWELVE-MONTH PERIOD 2014–15[a]

	Median	Mean
Total (all adults ≥18)	4	12
Gender		
Male	3	9
Female	5	14
Ethnicity		
White, Non-Hispanic	5	13
Black, Non-Hispanic	3	8
Hispanic	2	8
Age		
18–29	4	11
30–49	4	12
50–64	3	12
≥65	3	12
Level of Education		
High school graduate or less	1	7
Some college	5	13
College+	7	17

SOURCE: *Pew Research Center (2015c).*

[a]Among all American adults ages 18+ (including nonreaders), the mean (average) and median (midpoint) number read in whole or in part by each group.

CHAPTER 2

Sampling and Generalizability

Critical Thinking, Step Two: Who participated in the research, and how was the sample of respondents selected? When looking at information, reading reports, and evaluating research, it's critical to know who participated. Are you confident enough that the number and type of respondents are appropriate for the focus of the study and for the conclusions drawn? Critical thinking involves using tools to evaluate good and inadequate samples in order to fully assess the accuracy of survey results, media reports, and research studies.

In 2016, polls predicted that the citizens of the United Kingdom would reject Brexit (the referendum to leave the European Union) and support staying in the EU. Polls also indicated a high probability that Hillary Clinton would win the U.S. presidential election over Donald Trump, even if the differences in polling between them were within the margin of error. For many complex reasons, the political surveys did not achieve the successes they have often had in the past. One key reason, however, had to do with issues related to who participated in the polls. These results did not mark the first time sampling was targeted as an explanation.

Remember the 32nd president of the United States, Alfred Landon? You don't? You know: the one the *Literary Digest*'s political poll said would beat Franklin Roosevelt in 1936? The magazine's claim was based on around 2.3 million people; surely that was a large enough sample to generate accurate data, especially when compared with the 1,000 or so people who respond to today's polls. Of course, we now know that Roosevelt won that election (and two more after it) and that the *Literary Digest* was out of business by 1938. What went wrong in their polling prediction?

Explanations focus on problems with the sampling: Some have said that the magazine depended on car registration lists and phone books to construct the sample, biasing the results toward higher income groups, who tended to favor the Republican candidate. Others (e.g., Squire, 1988) argue that it was the small, biased sample of returned ballots that caused the wrong prediction: Fewer than 25 percent of those receiving ballots responded; nonresponse bias occurred when those who did not return their ballots were more likely to be Roosevelt supporters. Pollsters today also make a more refined distinction—among (a) the general adult population, (b) registered voters, and (c) likely voters—when conducting election surveys, something the *Literary Digest* did not do. Larger sample sizes do not, on their own, guarantee accurate results. And as witnessed in the 2016 U.S. presidential election, polling has become a problematic predictor of outcomes.

When the original population from which a subset of respondents is drawn is not clearly defined and is not representative of that population's diversity, samples are unlikely to achieve accurate information about opinions or behavior. Statisticians have developed random probability techniques to ensure that samples reflect the population and to reasonably conclude that polling about 1,000 people will result in findings accurate to within a margin of error of plus or minus 3 percent. (See chapter 1.)

Many times we make decisions about everyday issues based on a nonscientific survey of friends. Think about how you pleaded with a parent, "Everybody is going to the concert; why can't I?" despite the absence of survey results conducted randomly to bolster your claim. Or consider how you get recommendations for movies, restaurants, or travel. You ask people you know, or maybe read a restaurant guidebook or comments found on a website like Yelp or Trip Advisor. None of these is in any way more representative of opinions than the questionable polls you can find on various news websites with hundreds of thousands of voters expressing their views. In fact, many online polls add "This is not a scientific poll" when you click for the results, since an instant survey depends on who reads that website, who happened to be there when the poll was posted, and who decides to opt in to complete the (typically one-question) survey.

Asking a few people's opinions is reasonable when deciding whether to forage for the perfect pizza, but it is not a method you should use exclusively if you have to make life-or-death decisions about health issues or public policy.

ANECDOTAL SAMPLES

Nearly every day Internet blogs, television advertisements, and book and movie newspaper blurbs supply us with testimonies and praises for products that will change our lives. Just go to any website pushing some new weight loss scheme or a remedy to cure baldness to see how great a part anecdotes play in convincing people to part with their money. Consider this African Mango Diet Pill ad (which has since been removed from the Internet): "David J. says 'I've always been skeptical of diet products, but I had to give this one a try after seeing it on TV. WOW! I've already lost 4 inches of stomach fat and 18 pounds!'" Yet, not nearly as much as "Kate K.," who, in the same ad, claims losing 23 pounds thanks to "such a great product that really WORKS!"

Are two people ($n = 2$ in statistical notation) enough to convince you to purchase that product? What about one person, such as celebrity doctor Mehmet Oz, who promotes several weight-loss products, basing his recommendations on studies primarily using anecdotal data or faulty research designs? On his television show, Dr. Oz claimed, "You may think magic is make-believe, but this little bean has scientists saying they've found the magic weight loss cure for every body type: It's green coffee extract" and "I've got the number-one miracle in a bottle to burn your fat: It's raspberry ketone" (Hamblin, 2014).

Called in 2014 before a congressional hearing on deceptive advertising, Dr. Oz admitted to extolling the "miracle" aspects of alternative remedies as a way of motivating his viewers to do something about their health. Critical thinking, however, involves uncovering the sampling methods used in supposedly scientific studies that apparently depend on anecdotal accounts of effectiveness.

Anecdotal evidence is data collected from small, often biased samples chosen to support some claim or product, is not collected systematically with reliable and valid measurements, and usually implies causal connections. (See chapter 5.) It is often personal testimony, which depends on people providing narratives supporting or refuting some belief. There is nothing inherently wrong in gathering qualitative data—responses and narratives—unless the sample is specifically being chosen to bias the anecdotes in favor of or in opposition to the researchers' objectives. The lack of scientific consistency and the absence of systematic methods when collecting anecdotal evidence (along with the bias in finding just the right respondents to tell their stories) are what need to be critically assessed when reading or hearing claims made about a supposedly scientific study. (See chapter 6 for a discussion of the scientific method in contrast to the use of anecdotes and testimonies.)

CRITICAL THINKING TIP

Analyze whether the claims presented appear in one direction that may be too good to be true, are based on only a few respondents, and sound like endorsements or testimonial anecdotes. See whether data from scientific studies are presented using valid and reliable methodology, and inquire whether the studies were financed by the sponsors or makers of the products.

What's required in thinking critically about data presented in reports, studies, the media, and academic research is a careful questioning of the sampling methodology. Let's look at three sampling characteristics that are necessary to consider when critically evaluating research. First, review the *sampling type* to determine whether it is the best one for the research goals. Is the sample representative of the population for the purpose of the study? Is a true random sampling required? Second, ask about the *sample relevancy;* that is, are the *units of analysis* (the "who" or "what" being sampled) appropriate for the goals of the research? Third, see if the *sample size* and the number of observations are sufficient for making the best conclusions.

SAMPLE TYPES

Here is a well-known case of the media reporting a study that was later discovered to be based on a faulty sample. The Associated Press (AP) circulated the results of a poll conducted by the American Medical Association (AMA) with these words: "The AMA-commissioned online survey queried a nationwide random sample of 644 college women or graduates ages 17 to 35." The AP said 83 percent of the sample claimed that spring break involves heavier-than-usual drinking, and 74 percent said it also led to an increase in sexual activity. Of the 27 percent who had gone on a spring break trip, more than half regretted getting sick from drinking. The AMA reported the survey as having a margin of error of plus or minus 4 percent at the 95 percent level of confidence.

However, it became clear after some investigation that this was not a random sample but a nonprobability volunteer one (Blumenthal, 2006).

The *New York Times* (Rosenthal, 2006) printed a correction after it published an article about the AMA study: "The sample, it turned out, was not random. It included only women who volunteered to answer questions—and only a quarter of them had actually ever taken a spring break trip. They hardly constituted a reliable cross-section, and there is no way to calculate a margin of sampling error for such a 'sample.'"

Not only did the media sensationalize the results in a "girls-gone-wild" depiction; they also focused on the finding from the 27 percent who actually had been on a spring break trip as if they represented all college women. In other words, they generalized to the entire population from a nonrandom sample whose margin of error cannot be determined. *Generalization* refers to how well the findings of a study can be used to represent the population from which the sample was drawn. Generalizability is usually acceptable from a random sample; otherwise, you can report only that the results are limited to those sampled. That was the *Literary Digest*'s error, as well as the AMA's.

Let's look at various types of sampling methods and understand why these studies had problems with how their results were interpreted.

Random Probability Sampling

What does it mean to refer to a sample as "random"? Hanging out in a shopping mall and asking random people walking by? Handing out surveys randomly to students walking into the school cafeteria? Putting a survey on your Facebook page, inviting people to fill it in and to randomly share it with their friends?

That's a word used casually all the time but without the precision required in doing research. According to Hiebert (2011):

Random is without pattern or objective; it's perfectly unbiased. To judge by the pop-culture usages . . ., however, the word has shifted away from its traditional usage, and now means:

a. inconsequential

b. rare, strange, curated

c. exciting, absurd, capricious

d. unexpected, arbitrary, silly

e. outcast, distasteful, unknown

f. unlikely, unfeasible, impossible

g. incongruous fun

When it comes to reading research and interpreting findings from a quantitative survey or poll, it's essential to determine whether the investigators used a random sampling method. Generalizing to a larger population from which a sample is drawn requires *probability sampling*: that is, a sample in which every element has an equal (or known) chance of being selected. (Chapter 3 discusses the concept of probability in more detail.)

Making accurate inferences, with small margins of error, about a population from a random sample is the goal of most quantitative research. Yet, critical thinking requires looking out for other kinds of errors, such as the *ecological fallacy*. In this case, making conclusions about an individual based on data analyzed at the group level, regardless of the random sampling, is problematic. If exit polls in an election indicated that 56 percent of 18- to 24-year-olds voted for the Democratic candidate, concluding that your 20-year-old cousin voted that way is an ecological fallacy. *Can you find examples of such false logic in social media comments and Facebook postings?*

Generating random samples, however, requires having access to a population or sampling frame that can be readily defined. Various random sampling methods exist (systematic, stratified, multistage, random digit dialing), each resulting in the ability to estimate findings about the population within a specified margin of error and confidence limit. These types vary in how they obtain the random sample: *Systematic* depends on selecting every *n*th person after a random start; *stratified* defines categories first (like gender or age groupings) within which random samples are selected; *multistage* sampling depends on defining clusters at each stage, like randomly selecting regions of the country at the first stage, then randomly choosing states within those regions in the second stage, and finally randomly selecting school districts within those states at the third stage (Nardi, 2014).

Many research companies (such as Gallup, Pew, Nielsen, National Opinion Research Center) depend on random sampling and offer information on their websites about obtaining representative groups to poll and survey. Somewhat debated in the polling field is the accuracy of obtaining random and representative samples when using online Internet surveys and phone calls, especially when landlines are becoming less common than mobile cell phones. For example, Pew Research Center (2016a) describes their *random digit dialing* sampling for phone surveys as follows:

A majority of Pew Research Center surveys are conducted among the U.S. general public by telephone using a sampling method known as random digit dialing or "RDD." This method ensures that all telephone numbers in the U.S—whether landline or cellphone—have a known chance of being included. As a result, samples based on RDD should be unbiased, and a margin of sampling error and a confidence level can be computed for them.

The *New York Times* pollsters believe live telephone surveys of a random sample of Americans are the best way to measure public opinion (Broder, 2016):

> The polling establishment—including the 40-year-old New York Times/CBS News Poll—has viewed online polling with skepticism because it is difficult to achieve a random national sample using online interviews. There are also questions about how self-selected (so-called opt-in) respondents may differ from a truly random sample of the public. It is also impossible, so far at least, to calculate a margin of sampling error for an online-only population sample.

Yet, pollsters are beginning to explore the use of online surveys as the *New York Times* did by first getting a random probability sample and then offering respondents with an Internet connection the opportunity to complete it online, whereas those participants without access were interviewed by telephone. In general, however, online surveys are more characteristic of nonprobability sampling. *With increasing nonresponse rates in telephone and written surveys, how much different will random probability sampling be from online surveys in the future?*

Nonprobability Sampling

Many people often claim results, report important findings, and sometimes make decisions based on nonrandom, nonprobability samples that are completed by volunteers or readily available subjects, or through snowball methods. Margins of error cannot be adequately calculated for nonrandom samples, and this type limits generalizability beyond those units making up the sample.

Consider this media report. A *New York Times* headline claims: "1 in 4 Women Experience Sex Assault on Campus" (Pérez-Peña, 2015). The opening paragraph clarifies this as meaning "undergraduate women at a large group of leading universities" but exclaims later on that this study "stands out for its sheer size—150,000 students at 27 colleges and universities." It is only about halfway into the story that we find out "only 19 percent of students responded to the survey" at that limited number of institutions. Remember the problems with the "spring break" sampling mentioned earlier?

In other words, the headline for this news item should more accurately read: "1 in 4 Women *of the 19 percent of undergraduates who actually responded to a survey at a nonrandom selection of colleges and universities* Experienced Sex Assault on Campus." What started out seemingly generalized to all women, then to undergrads only at leading colleges, in fact could rightfully be applied just to this selected, volunteer sample. It really doesn't matter if the sheer size is 150,000 at 27 colleges. As with the *Literary Digest* fiasco, size here doesn't matter. Since this is a sample of women who volunteered to complete the survey, we can make conclusions only about this particular set of respondents. It is a nonprobability sample that cannot be used to estimate a margin of error, let alone information about women in colleges and universities.

CRITICAL THINKING TIP

When interpreting findings from polls and research studies, review carefully whether the results are based on a random sample, and if not, see whether the reporting of the findings is being incorrectly generalized to a larger population than those units (people, colleges, etc.) making up the sample.

Convenience samples are quite common in informal polls, student projects for a class, or sometimes even in professional marketing research when random sampling is not possible. As the name suggests, research employing volunteers (opt-in subjects) or easily accessible units of analysis is very convenient but not necessarily representative of a larger population. Here are several examples of nonprobability convenience sampling:

- Distributing surveys to an introductory political science class cannot be generalized to all students at the college or to all political science students or even to that particular class, especially if many decided not to attend on that rainy Monday when they were given out!
- The Sunday *New York Times Magazine* weekly survey conducted online with "subscribers who chose to participate."

- Standing outside the movie theater and asking the first 35 men and 35 women to respond to your questions about a film is not sufficient to generalize to the opinions of all male and female moviegoers, even though a *quota* sample was used to balance the responses.

- Analyzing the current month's editorials in several local newspapers about their positions on how to deal with worldwide terrorism may not be generalizable to all the views in today's media, given the convenience of looking only at what's easily available in the local paper or website.

- Getting in touch with members of the LGBT Center and requesting them to pass along a questionnaire to other LGBT people they know is called *snowball* or chain-referral sampling, but this sampling type does not necessarily mean the results are representative of all LGBT people in the community, city, state, or country.

This chain-referral nonprobability sampling can be a useful technique in generating a sample, as Canadian researchers (Tremblay and Sauvêtre, 2014) did to find juvenile car thieves to be interviewed about their delinquency career (age started, arrests, convictions, connections with other thieves, family background, etc.). Focus was not on uncovering causal explanations; rather, the goal was to describe the patterns and profiles of young car thieves.

Given the difficulty of obtaining a random sample of all offenders, the researchers began by having students taking their course use their friendship networks to find youth involved in stealing cars. (See fig. 1.) In the first round, they found four car thieves; three of these four offenders in turn recruited eight more (youth number 4, for example, got offenders numbered 10, 11, and 12; youth number 12 found number 25, etc.). After four waves, 34 car thieves became part of their sample.

The authors did not generalize beyond these people to all youth offenders or juvenile car thieves, and they avoided making any causal explanations or statistical analyses in recognition that their sampling method was not random.

Each of these examples is a nonprobability sample, since not every unit of analysis (editorials, LGBT members, moviegoers, introductory political science students, and car thieves) has an equal chance of being selected for the research study. Sampling focused only on the most

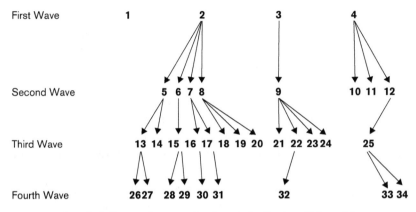

FIGURE 1. Snowball diagram for a sample of car-theft offenders. (Adapted from Tremblay and Sauvêtre, 2014: 171.)

convenient units (those students who showed up that day to class, the current month's editorials, etc.) does not provide margins of error, and it limits what we can say to only the units studied.

SAMPLE RELEVANCY

Once you determine the sampling method chosen, it's equally important to critically ask if it's the most appropriate one for the goals and topic of the research. Sometimes a random sample may not be the most relevant for the purposes of the study. *Qualitative* research, for example, typically involves nonquantitative in-depth ethnographic methods using observation, interviews, participant observation, case studies, and the creation of detailed field notes.

In order to generate questions for a later study on nutrition and diet plans, for example, researchers may ask participants attending a Weight Watchers program to keep a detailed food diary of what they eat at each meal. This sampling would not be appropriate to compare diet plans, to see if Weight Watchers is a cause of subjects' weight loss, or to make predictions about future eating patterns. Nonprobability techniques are typically more useful in exploratory and qualitative research when the goals are not primarily to explain, predict, or prove causation.

Nonprobability *focus groups* are relevant in an early stage of exploratory research, when trying to understand the language, topics, and concerns of a particular target population. Robinson (1999: 906) puts it this way: "The aim of the method is therefore not to reach a generalized or representative statement of opinions, as with surveys where responses are limited. The assumption of focus group methodology is that opinions are not always readily available, and are open to influence by others in an interactive setting."

One typical situation in which focus groups are relevant is when gathering qualitative data for needs assessments of a social service program and to evaluate its effectiveness. Around five to ten people may be specifically invited to participate in a discussion about what the agency is doing well, what services clients expect to receive from the program, and what barriers may exist to receiving help from the agency.

Focus groups are also a relevant choice in generating strategies for a quantitative study later on. For example, a consulting firm was interested in understanding what motivates employees to do great work. To find out, researchers conducted some qualitative and quantitative studies with companies across the country. Here is why they decided to use focus groups first (Kaufman, Christensen, and Newton, 2015: 3):

> These focus groups played an integral role in the development of our quantitative research. It was during these focus groups that we confirmed the type of motivating perks and practices organizations use to encourage employees, how effective employees perceived those perks and practices to be, and how to best frame the quantitative survey to produce unbiased results.

CRITICAL THINKING TIP

Don't just review the type of sampling used; also assess whether the units of analysis are those most relevant for the research topic. Ask whether another sampling method and different subjects would have been better choices for the goals of the study under review. Is the purpose of the study at an exploratory stage? Or is it to seek out explanations of cause-and-effect relationships?

Sometimes researchers need to generate a relevant sample selected on purpose in order to explore a specific topic. Leaving it up to the judgment of the researchers, this nonprobability method is called *purposive or judgmental* sampling. It involves choosing participants who meet the relevant goals of the research. For example, in order to understand "why first-generation Chinese immigrants with diabetes have difficulty obtaining, processing and understanding diabetes related information despite the existence of translated materials and translators," researchers (Leung et al., 2014) generated a sample "through purposive sampling. Participants were eligible if they were: (1) first-generation Chinese immigrants living in Los Angeles County, (2) aged ≥45 years, and (3) diagnosed with type 2 diabetes for at least one year. Recruitment was conducted in regions highly populated by Chinese residents."

While a random sample might have similarly turned up Chinese immigrants 45 and older with diabetes, it would take a very large and expensive sampling process to do so. And like any nonprobability sampling, generalizing to all Chinese immigrants 45 and older with diabetes is not possible. Conclusions drawn from this study are limited to the 29 people purposely chosen for this research project.

Theoretical reasons and prior research typically contribute to deciding the type of sampling methods to use and to choosing the most relevant participants to select for a study or survey. But often practical and financial reasons determine how many units of analysis are needed for a project.

SAMPLE SIZE

Critical thinking requires asking whether the sample size is appropriate for the research. A gold standard of probability sampling is usually to generate a random sample of around 1,000 units of analysis that lends itself to a margin of error of 3 percent. See for yourself how the random sample size changes once you determine the number in the population that you are studying and after you decide on the margin of error you are comfortable with at a particular confidence level (usually 95% or 99%). *Survey Monkey* has an online calculator that provides various ways to compare this information: https://www.surveymonkey.com /mp/sample-size-calculator/.

Most professional survey organizations balance accuracy and cost by settling on sample sizes of 1,000. The National Council on Public Polls (Gawiser and Witt, n.d.) states:

> Interviews with a scientific sample of 1,000 adults can accurately reflect the opinions of nearly 210 million American adults. That means interviews attempted with all 210 million adults—if such were possible—would give approximately the same results as a well-conducted survey based on 1,000 interviews. What happens if another carefully done poll of 1,000 adults gives slightly different results from the first survey? Neither of the polls is "wrong." This range of possible results is called the error due to sampling, often called

the margin of error. This is not an "error" in the sense of making a mistake. Rather, it is a measure of the possible range of approximation in the results because a sample was used.

Another issue in deciding sample size is how much you intend to break down the findings into subgroups. If you wish to compare people (1) under 30, (2) between 30 and 60, and (3) over 60, ask if there are enough subjects in each of those three categories to make meaningful comparisons. Many research companies use statistical weighting to adjust sample sizes of subgroups to be more representative of the larger population or to adjust for smaller demographic categories of under-represented groups. For example (Gallup, 2016):

> Gallup weights samples to correct for unequal selection probability and non-response. Gallup also weights its final samples to match the U.S. population according to gender, age, race, Hispanic ethnicity, education, and region. Demographic weighting targets are based on the most recent Current Population Survey figures for the aged 18 and older U.S. population.

What is less clear is the size needed for nonprobability samples or qualitative research. Since statistical inferences about a larger population are not possible with convenience, snowball, or purposive samples, size is best determined by how many you think you will minimally need to achieve your goals. Are you gathering enough information with 29 Chinese immigrants 45 and older with Type 2 diabetes, or do you need, say, more women or more men in the study? Using a *quota* sample (the non-probability version of a stratified random probability sample) is one method of getting enough units to analyze in each of the subcategories.

For example, a study (Wartberg et al., 2014) conducted in Germany focusing on compulsive Internet use among 14- to 17-year-olds opted for a quota sample in which each age would make up 25 percent of the sample (that is, 25% 14-year-olds, 25% 15-year-olds, etc.) and, within each age category, 50 percent split between males and females. The sample ended up with a total of 1,744 teens, with 218 males and 218 females in each of the four age groups. For their project's goals, these numbers allowed the researchers to break down the sample into relevant subcategories, even though it was not a random sample.

It's important to use your critical thinking tools and constructive skepticism in evaluating sampling methodologies. Be especially aware of anecdotal sampling: Like the mountebanks of old pushing their wondrous elixirs, testimonials from a few end up substituting for the scientific sampling of the many. Yet, it's not always practical to generate a random sample each time you need to find a great hotel or restaurant; just use your critical thinking skills when interpreting all those website opinions. De Langhe, Fernbach, and Lichtenstein (2016: 818), for example, found that average reviewer ratings of over 1,200 products on Amazon.com correlate poorly with quality ratings of the same products evaluated by *Consumer Reports*. People tend to ignore the insufficient sample size of online reviews; price and brand name seem to be stronger determinants of higher online ratings.

Other nonprobability sampling methods can be sufficient, depending on the goals of the study. Critically assess the research questions and decide whether the type of sampling selected can answer those questions, whether the composition of the sample is relevant to answering them, and whether there is a sufficient number of units in the sample to be able to analyze the data in multiple ways.

ETHICS AND CONSENT

Imagine a study designed to compare treatments for a terminal disease. One sample of participants would receive the medication required to halt the illness while another sample of subjects does not get any treatment (or takes some placebo sugar pill). *At first hearing about this study as a critical thinker, what concerns would you raise?* Imagine, then, that neither group was informed whether they actually had the disease or not. *What issues would you now raise?* Imagine that a cure was found to work, but neither group received that medication, so that researchers could learn more about how the disease progresses when untreated. *If you were evaluating this research, what ethical guidelines would you invoke to decide whether your review board would approve it for funding?*

Difficult as it is to imagine such a scenario, the Tuskegee Study of Untreated Syphilis in the Negro Male in 1932 reflected this kind of research design. Begun under the guidance of the U.S. Public Health Service, the goal was to investigate the natural progression of syphilis in black men (Centers for Disease Control and Prevention, 2016):

> The study initially involved 600 black men—399 with syphilis, 201 who did not have the disease. The study was conducted without the benefit of patients' informed consent. Researchers told the men they were being treated for "bad blood," a local term used to describe several ailments, including syphilis, anemia, and fatigue. In truth, they did not receive the proper treatment needed to cure their illness. In exchange for taking part in the study, the men received free medical exams, free meals, and burial insurance.

Although originally projected to last 6 months, the study actually went on for 40 years.

These men were misled about the project (being told not that they had been diagnosed with syphilis, but instead only some blood illness), were never given the opportunity to withdraw, and never received penicillin when it was discovered to be a cure for the disease, in 1947. Wives, children, and others were also infected and died over the years as a result of not being treated. When the media uncovered the study, in 1972, the project was halted, too late for the 100 or more men and women who had died. By 1975, the Tuskegee Health Benefit Program began to treat the remaining men and family members. This disastrous and unethical research resulted in the creation of federal guidelines and principles for conducting ethical research.

Critically reviewing how researchers select samples, ask questions, and design studies also involves evaluating the ethics of doing the research. Universities, professional organizations, and research institutes have codes of ethics governing the collection of data. Typically, an institutional review board (IRB) is set up to read the proposed research and investigate the ethical issues of the research design (the sampling, how the variables are measured, the methods of data collection and analysis, and how the findings will be used and distributed). It's also important to ask who is sponsoring the research and whether there are any conflicts of interest.

When human subjects are involved, codes of ethics emphasize that participants should not intentionally be physically or mentally harmed and that their right to privacy must be respected. When reading studies or hearing about research, critically review whether the participants have been given *informed consent*. This involves telling the subjects about any potential dangers and about the impact of the research design. *Are they participating free of coercion, and do they have the right to refuse answering some questions or engaging in some research conditions?*

> **CRITICAL THINKING TIP**
>
> Review the ethics of doing the study: Was the sample selected without coercion? Did participants give informed consent? Are their responses confidential or anonymous? Did the subjects continue to participate of their own free will? Evaluate the research in terms of autonomy, beneficence, and justice.

Ethical and consent issues require informing human subjects if their participation is confidential or anonymous. *Confidentiality* means that respondents could be linked to their specific answers but that their identities are revealed only to the researchers if needed (for example, with longitudinal studies, requiring following the participants over time). *Anonymity* is said to occur when there is no way of connecting any particular identifying information with any individual completing the study; respondents do not give any names or use code numbers connected to their names. "Confidentiality is not the same as anonymity: Anonymous information is always confidential since it can never personally be traced back to anyone, but confidential information is never anonymous since it is known who completed the survey" (Nardi, 2014: 38).

The key ethical guidelines for the protection of human subjects of research revolve around the principles of autonomy, beneficence, and justice (Belmont Report, 1979). Critically evaluating studies includes analyzing whether the researchers attended to these principles:

- *Autonomy* is the principle of respect for individuals as autonomous agents and protection of those with diminished autonomy (such as the incapacitated, the mentally ill, or prisoners). Participants in research must voluntarily participate on the basis of adequate information to consent to their involvement in the project.
- *Beneficence* requires researchers to do no harm, to maximize the benefits to knowledge and society, and to minimize the risks and potential injuries to the participants.
- *Justice* refers to fairness in distribution so that no particular group of people is systematically denied equal entitlement to a benefit or selected for participation in a research project because of their easy availability and manipulability, especially when unrelated to the purposes of the study.

This statement from the American Sociological Association's (2008: Principle D) *Code of Ethics* says it succinctly:

Sociologists respect the rights, dignity, and worth of all people. They strive to eliminate bias in their professional activities, and they do not tolerate any forms of discrimination based on age; gender; race; ethnicity; national origin; religion; sexual orientation; disability; health conditions; or marital, domestic, or parental status. They are sensitive to cultural, individual, and role differences in serving, teaching, and studying groups of people with distinctive characteristics. In all of their work-related activities, sociologists acknowledge the rights of others to hold values, attitudes, and opinions that differ from their own.

Evaluating the appropriateness of the sampling types, sampling size, and sampling units for the research questions being investigated, and determining how ethically these were selected, illustrate critical thinking.

KEY TERMS

ANECDOTAL SAMPLING Collecting data from small, often biased samples chosen to support some claim or product.

ANONYMITY The condition of data collection without any particular information identifying individuals completing a study.

ETHICS Principles ensuring that autonomy, beneficence, and justice are followed in research with participants' informed consent without coercion.

CONFIDENTIALITY The condition of data collection whereby respondents could be linked to their specific answers but are reassured that their identities are revealed only to the researchers and only if needed.

CONVENIENCE SAMPLING Nonprobability method of selecting respondents who are readily available to participate, sometimes on a volunteer basis.

ECOLOGICAL FALLACY Making conclusions about individuals based on information from group data.

FOCUS GROUPS Moderator-led collections of respondents discussing opinions about a topic, often guided by a set of questions.

GENERALIZABILITY A measure of how well the findings of a study can be used to represent a population from which a sample was drawn.

INFORMED CONSENT Respondents' choice to take part in a study based on being provided sufficient information to decide whether to participate in the research.

INSTITUTIONAL REVIEW BOARDS Committees evaluating the ethics related to the methodology and sampling of the research project.

MULTISTAGE SAMPLING A probability method of randomly selecting units of analysis at each of several stages.

NONPROBABILITY SAMPLING A method of selecting units of analysis in which all units in a population do not have an equal chance of being selected.

PURPOSIVE/JUDGMENTAL SAMPLING Researcher's selection of participants based on some specific characteristic or specialty needed for a study.

QUOTA SAMPLING A nonprobability method of selecting units of analysis in some designated proportion.

RANDOM DIGIT DIALING (RDD) Telephoning a random computer-generated set of phone numbers used in contacting respondents.

RANDOM PROBABILITY SAMPLING A method of selecting units of analysis in which every unit in the population has a specified, often equal chance of being selected for participation in a study.

SNOWBALL SAMPLING Nonprobability method of chain-referral in which participants are asked to suggest other possible respondents.

STRATIFIED SAMPLING A probability method that determines categories first and then randomly selects units within those groupings.

SYSTEMATIC SAMPLING A probability method using a random starting point and then selecting every person based on a fixed periodic interval.

EXERCISES

1. (a) A *Washington Examiner* newspaper headline read: "74% of small businesses will fire workers, cut hours under Obamacare" (Bedard, 2013). The story reported on a United States Chamber of Commerce–sponsored survey about the Affordable Care Act's employer mandate, conducted by the Harris Interactive polling company. The 74 percent figure was picked up by many media outlets and politicians. The Harris Interactive (2013: 1) report claimed: "Margin of sampling error: +/- 2.5 percentage points" for the 499 Chamber of Commerce members and 805 nonmember small business executives who completed the nonrandom opt-in online survey.

   (i) What would you say to the claim that the results are a scientific sample generalizable to all small businesses in the United States?

   (ii) What can you say about the margin of error for this nonrandom opt-in online survey?

   (b) Sampling became another source of controversy about this study. Harris Interactive (2013) stated the results about the requirement that an employer must provide health insurance if the company has 50 or more employees working full-time in this way: "Despite the Administration's delay of the employer mandate by a year, small businesses expect the requirement to negatively impact their employees. 27% say they will cut hours to reduce full time employees, 24% will reduce hiring, and 23% plan to replace full time employees (30 hours per week or more) with part-time workers to avoid triggering the mandate." Note that these percentages do add up to 74% as reported in the headline.

   However, the United States Chamber of Commerce (2013) press release stated it this way: "Among small businesses that will be impacted by the employer mandate, one-half of small businesses say that they will either cut hours to reduce full time employees OR replace full time employees with part-timers to avoid the mandate. 24% say they will reduce hiring to stay under 50 employees."

When critically reviewing the original survey, you learn that the survey asked this question first—*Will you be impacted by the employer mandate?*—and then provided five possible answers (cut hours, replace employees, etc., and included "none of the above") with the instructions *Please select all that apply*:

    (i) What does the phrase "among small businesses that will be impacted by the employer mandate" tell you about which sample data are being reported, especially when you learn that only 17 percent said yes, they would be impacted.

   (ii) What does "Please select all that apply" tell you about the way the numbers are presented and added up to get 74 percent?

  (iii) Rewrite the original newspaper headline to reflect what the study actually says.

2. A researcher for a manufacturing company with 18,000 employees wanted to specifically survey those who had worked at the place for 10 or more years. The company's Human Resources Department provided a list of 12,452 people who qualified. Using a sample size calculator, the researcher determined she needed 373 participants to get a margin of error of 5 percent with a 95 percent confidence level. So she sends out surveys to all 12,452 people and receives 623 back.

As a critically thinking consultant hired by the company to review the study, what would you say about the sample? Is it enhanced for achieving more than was needed? Does this change the margin of error and confidence level? To whom can she generalize with the results from this sample?

3. A journalist was curious about her fellow newspaper folks who were laid off or bought out from their journalism jobs and what they were doing now. So she posted a questionnaire online at various journalist-related websites and received 595 completed surveys. She acknowledged that "This was not a scientific poll, because there is no comprehensive list of those who've been laid off from which to draw a random sample" (Hodierne, 2009).

(a) Using the concepts from this chapter about sample type, sample relevancy, and sample size, review his methodology and say to whom you can generalize the findings.

(b) As a consultant, design a sampling plan for another study to explore this same research question about life after a career in journalism.

4. You find yourself on an Institutional Review Board. Discuss what may be ethical issues in the following research proposals:

(a) Students in a high school are asked to volunteer for a study on eating habits and diets.

(b) A survey about drug use in respondents' families is to be given to people in a rehabilitation clinic. Those who participate will receive $20.

(c) You set up a Facebook page describing yourself with a race and age different from your own in order to study how people react to your postings about political topics.

(d) The proposal is to go to a fitness center or gym and observe and take notes how people of different weights use the equipment and exercise.

CHAPTER 3

Probability and Coincidence

Critical Thinking, Step Three: What role does probability play in what you are reading, reviewing, and interpreting? So much information in the media can be critically evaluated knowing more about coincidence and probability. Consider the odds when assessing risks confronted in everyday situations and as reported on social media. Review the statistical significance of quantitative academic research findings that use probability concepts. This chapter provides the tools to ask how likely what is being claimed can happen by chance alone before any conclusions and decisions are reached.

You know it's your lucky day, so you decide to buy a Powerball lottery ticket. Select your six numbers such as 1, 2, 3, 4, 5, and 6. But you'll never know if you won, because on your way home you get hit by an asteroid or maybe struck by lightning. You failed to consider these probabilities: the odds of getting all six numbers are around 1 in 293,000,000, but the odds of being killed by an asteroid are only 1 in 1,600,000 (Howard, 2016). And for getting hit by lightning, the odds are 1 in 135,000.

If you're like most people, you tend to let emotion take over from rational and mathematical thinking. See how some people react when you choose six numbers in a row: "You'll never win. The winning numbers never are in order." You can tell people only so many times that the numbers don't know they are sequential and the odds are the same for any six ordered numbers as they are for six randomly selected out-of-sequence ones. Yet, understanding the probability of phenomena occurring is a key element of critical thinking and social science research. Not only are statistics evaluated using probability thresholds; so is much of everyday life.

Let's consider several different ways of understanding probability: coincidental, mathematical, and statistical. Use these concepts as critical tools when evaluating what you are hearing or reading in social media, in print, and in scholarly publications.

COINCIDENTAL

A colleague excitedly told the story about running into a former student while walking around Tokyo. How often does that happen? What a coincidence! Admit it: You feel this too when you, out of the blue, receive a text from someone you were just thinking about and have not heard from recently. The noted psychiatrist Carl Jung called this phenomenon *synchronicity* or *meaningful coincidence,* two events linked by some shared meaning even without a causal connection. Thinking about someone does not cause that person to contact you, but it does appear to have some shared meaning.

The probability of such coincidences seems pretty low. This perception, however, may be false, based on human social psychology. Let's apply some critical thinking to such phenomena. We tend to seek logical or sometimes even paranormal, religious, or superstitious explanations for events that seem rarely to occur. We engage in *selective perception* and *selective retention,* whereby we notice some elements of an event while disattending others and remembering later on only certain aspects of that event. So much of people's experiences with psychics depends on their selectively hearing what is being said and selectively recalling what they earlier heard. Many times they attribute to the psychic what they themselves told the psychic (Hines, 2003).

Consider this classic experiment illustrating what may seem like a coincidence. Forer (1949) had students complete a personality test, and a week later they received a written assessment of their results. Forer asked them to rate the accuracy of their personality profiles; the result was very high ratings (an average of 4.26, where 5 was designated "very accurate"). What a coincidence that all the evaluations appeared to be so accurate! Or was it? Each person in fact received the exact same assessment that Forer (1949: 120) took from a newspaper horoscope: "You have a great need for other people to like and admire you. You have a tendency to be critical of yourself. While you have some personality weaknesses, you are generally able to compensate for them. . . . You pride yourself as an independent thinker and do not accept others' statements without satisfactory proof." *How well does that statement describe you too?*

What Forer discovered was that people often accept vague and general statements as accurate about themselves without the benefit of any objective measurement. When empirically false statements sound positive, they will agree that the traits describe them accurately. This selective perception is sometimes called *the Forer effect* or *subjective validation*. What may appear as coincidence is in reality a common social psychological process of *confirmation bias:* ignoring conflicting information and focusing only on those dimensions that reinforce views already held.

More important than horoscopes is how we tend to selectively choose media sources that illustrate a confirmation bias. As a Pew Research Center study found: "When it comes to getting news about politics and government, liberals and conservatives inhabit different worlds. There is little overlap in the news sources they turn to and trust. And whether discussing politics online or with friends, they are more likely than others to interact with like-minded individuals" (Mitchell et al., 2014).

CRITICAL THINKING TIP

How are you using selective perception and confirmation bias when experiencing an event? Are you seeing only a limited range of what is available? Are you recalling only selective information that in many ways confirms already-held views? Apply the same questioning to the content in the research that you read, the social media that you engage with, and the news stories that you hear. Are these sources selectively making claims and reporting information?

Given these selective human processes, reconsider the odds of running into someone we know when far away from home. The *law of truly large numbers* suggests that with increasing number of cases, rare events are more likely to occur. Sure, we think narrowly of ourselves as one person running into one acquaintance on one street in one city on one particular day at one specific time. But if we rethink this one event in terms of a truly large number, such as all the acquaintances we do know in our social networks, all the streets there are in all the cities we visit, on all the days of the week, during all the hours of a particular day, we actually increase the probability of running into someone we know. How this increase happens is explained mathematically in the next section.

We selectively retell the story of accidentally seeing a familiar face in an unusual place, and in so doing we selectively ignore all the times when we did not meet a friend (let alone that person) on all the other streets walked in all those other cities on all the other days of the week.

In other words, coincidences and extreme events do happen, but their probability increases when you consider more than $N = 1$ and include a much larger number of possibilities.

MATHEMATICAL

Besides selective thinking, another reason why people exaggerate the probability of seeing an acquaintance in some location far from home is confusion between two characteristics of mathematical probability: *union* and *intersection*.

Let's begin with the probability of randomly selecting either one of two mutually exclusive events—that is, two events one of which cannot occur at the same time as the other. The two events are sometimes referred to as *disjoint*. Imagine you get to spin a wheel that has the numbers 1 through 5 on it. You cannot land on two numbers at the same time, because ending up on one number precludes landing on any other. The numbers on this wheel are mutually exclusive.

What, then, is the probability of landing on, say, the number 4? Out of five possible outcomes, there is only one chance for the spinning wheel to stop on the number 4, so the odds are 1 in 5 (1 divided by 5, or 0.20). And what is the probability of landing on the number 4 OR the number 2? Here the probability is the *union* of two chances, mathematically *adding* them, depicted as $P(A \text{ or } B) = P(A) + P(B)$. So the probability of getting a 4 *or* a 2 is $1/5 + 1/5 = 2$ in 5 (2/5 or 0.40). You have a 40 percent chance of spinning the wheel and landing on the number 2 *or* 4.

If the two events are not mutually exclusive and there is some overlap, mathematically you need to subtract the overlapping probability, depicted as $P(A \text{ or } B) = P(A) + P(B) - P(A \text{ and } B)$. For example, what is the probability of spinning the wheel and landing on a 3 *or* any odd number? Since 3 is also an odd number, there is some overlap in events. The odds of landing on a 3 are 1 in 5, and the odds of getting an odd number are 3 in 5 (the odd numbers 1, 3, 5).

But if you add up these odds to get 4 in 5, you are distorting the probability by not considering the fact that 3 is also an odd number, and you're counting it in two events that can happen at the same time. Since there is only one odd number out of five that is also a 3, you need to subtract 1/5 to end up with an overall probability of 3 out of 5. Using the formula: $1/5 + 3/5 - 1/5 = 3/5$ (or 0.60). The probability of landing on the 3 or any odd number is 60 percent.

Now, imagine you would win some big jackpot if you were to spin the wheel and get the same number twice in a row. This probability depends on the *intersection* of two independent events. The odds of landing on the number 2, for example, are 1 in 5 on your first spin. Since the numbers don't care what has happened before, the odds of getting the number 2 on a second spin remain 1 in 5. To determine the probability of intersecting events, you *multiply* the odds: $P(A \text{ and } B) = P(A) \times P(B)$. So, $1/5 \times 1/5 = 1$ in 25 ($1/25 = 0.04$). There is a 4 percent chance that you will spin the same number twice in a row. Three times in a row? $1/5 \times 1/5 \times 1/5 = 1/125$ (or 0.008). That's 0.8 percent of a chance, barely even a 1 percent chance of spinning the same number three times in a row.

CRITICAL THINKING TIP

Ask whether what you are reading or hearing is really that improbable. Using the rules of adding or multiplying probabilities, try to quickly estimate the odds of something happening. Also assess whether the claims and information are coincidental and dependent on there being truly large numbers involved.

In short, you add together (union) the probabilities when you are calculating the odds for any mutually exclusive events to occur. You multiply (intersection) the probabilities when you are calculating the odds for independent events to occur at the same time. Notice how the probabilities get smaller (or rarer) when you multiply, so winning the lottery is based on the intersection of six independent numbers happening simultaneously. Imagine how much easier it would be if you get one of your numbers picked in the lottery *or* for another one *or* for another one, and so on. It's more difficult to get all six at the same time.

So how does this connect to running into a friend on some street corner while traveling in another city? First you have to figure out how many acquaintances you have; how many streets there are; how many hours in the day; how many days you are traveling; how many cities you visit; and so forth. We have a tendency to see these coincidences as one in a million based on thinking of probabilities as intersections (one of our friends *and* on this street *and* in this city *and* at this hour— "What are the odds?!" you would exclaim).

However, these events are actually about mathematical union: the probability of seeing a friend *or* another friend *or* another friend at 1:00 P.M. *or* at 2:00 P.M. *or* in one city *or* another city, on one street *or* another street, and so on. What we have are increasing probabilities involving truly large numbers that at some point we will indeed run into someone we know coincidentally, seemingly randomly, somewhere at some time on some street in some city. After all, if you tell the person you're in a relationship with that "You're one in a million, Kiddo," this surely sounds like a compliment. But if you are living in the Tokyo metropolitan area, with its population of 38 million, there are 37 others as rare as your partner!

A brief aside here: We often get the words "odds" and "probabilities" mixed up. Colloquially, we might yell "What are the odds?!" when we mean "What is the probability?!" of this happening. Mathematically, they are calculated differently, even though they are both about the likelihood of something occurring. (See Dolinar, 2014.) A probability is a fraction calculated by dividing a desired outcome by all possible outcomes, resulting in some number between 0 and 1 (or, when multiplied by 100, between 0 percent and 100 percent). For example, selecting the five of diamonds from a pack of 52 cards is 1/52, or about 2 percent.

Odds are a ratio of the likelihood of an outcome occurring to the likelihood of that outcome not occurring. The odds, for example, of choosing an ace from a deck of cards would be 4 (likelihood of it occurring) to 48 (likelihood of it not occurring), represented with a colon, 4:48 (or 1:12). You would say 1:12 as "the odds are 1 to 12 that you will pick an ace." Sports often use odds in gambling bets. Yet, if you were speaking in terms of probability, you would instead say "the probability of picking an ace is 4 out of 52 chances, or a 7.7 percent probability." *What is the probability of getting heads when flipping a coin versus the odds of it coming up heads?*

STATISTICAL

Thinking critically entails putting everyday life events and coincidences into reasonable probability perspectives, and it also relates to interpreting research findings using statistics. So much of research involves answering the question whether what was found is significantly different from what could have resulted from chance alone.

Recall the discussion about confidence limits and margins of error. (See chapter 2.) A political poll, for example, reports that 43 percent of voters support a particular candidate, plus or minus 3 percent at the 95 percent confidence level. This means that out of 100 polls conducted on similar samples, we are sure that the actual results would be between 40 percent and 46 percent in 95 of those samples.

The same question can be posed with statistical results. Is the probability that in 95 out of 100 equivalent samples we would also obtain such a mean or correlation coefficient (or some other statistic) within plus or minus some relevant margin of error? If so, we declare that we have uncovered a *statistically significant* finding. This probability is presented as $p<.05$, the figure usually designated as the cut-off point for significance. For some studies, in order to be more confident in the findings, researchers can decide to declare significance only at or less than ($\leq$) the .01 or .001 probability level, especially in cases when the sample size is large. Analyses of so-called Big Data, which depend on massive amounts of information collected, can make small differences appear statistically more significant.

CRITICAL THINKING TIP

When reading or hearing about research, evaluate the significance level by reviewing the p values. Is this study important enough to require a higher standard, like $p<.01$ or $p<.001$, rather than the minimum, $p<.05$? Are conclusions being made that do not reflect the statistical significance?

What do these p values signify? These numbers represent the probability of getting the results by random sampling error. When statistical findings are significant at the .01 level, it means that if we had 100 samples, then in one of those samples, similar research findings could have occurred by chance alone. In other words, it would be a rare event to get such a result by chance, so something meaningful must be happening in the one sample we studied.

Take, for example, yet another media report of a "wonderful new diet plan." Imagine that you read that people in group A lost 25 pounds eating only kale and blueberries for six weeks, and those in group B lost 15 pounds drinking grapefruit juice and diet sodas during the same period. What is the likelihood that the ten pound difference could have been due to chance and not to the kale-blueberry diet? Statistical tests are performed (such as a t-test or a chi square), and probabilities are calculated. The smaller the probability is ($p<.05$ or $p<.01$, certainly $p<.001$), the smaller is the likelihood that random chance could explain the differences in diet plans between the two groups.

If the statistical tests for this study were significant with $p<.01$, we would declare a statistically significant finding and conclude that the new diet plan is doing its job. (Of course, in a real study, it would be necessary to control for all sorts of other factors that may have contributed to the weight loss in one group and lower weight loss in the other group.)

A p value of .01 tells us that the likelihood of getting such a difference in weight loss *by chance* is one random sample out of 100 samples; to put it another way, this p value means that there is a 99 percent probability of a difference in pounds lost between the two diet groups could be explained by the diet.

For the more statistically interested, what is being done logically is testing the *null hypothesis* of no difference in weight between the two groups in the population. We reject the null of no difference and declare a significant difference when the probability is less than 0.05 (or other set amount). A p value of .01, for example, tells us that if the new diet plan makes no difference, we would accidentally (because of random sampling error) get such a difference in just 1 percent of all possible samples when there really is none.

As Frost (2014) puts it:

> In every experiment, there is an effect or difference between groups that the researchers are testing. It could be the effectiveness of a new drug, building material, or other intervention that has benefits. Unfortunately for the researchers, there is always the possibility that there is no effect, that is, that there is no difference between the groups. This lack of a difference is called the null hypothesis, which is essentially the position a devil's advocate would take when evaluating the results of an experiment. . . . P values evaluate how well the sample data support the devil's advocate argument that the null hypothesis is true. It measures how compatible your data are with the null hypothesis. How likely is the effect observed in your sample data if the null hypothesis is true? . . . A low P value suggests that your sample provides enough evidence that you can reject the null hypothesis for the entire population.

Of course, discovering a statistically significant finding does not necessarily make it a meaningful one or cause you to rule out other factors more relevant to establishing a difference or causality. It is simply a guidepost in helping us think critically about research. Sciences, especially the social sciences, depend on probability. Rarely do we prove something: Science is an ongoing project, with results that are tentative until demonstrated otherwise. Chapter 6 presents more of this discussion on the process of scientific thinking.

COINCIDENCE, PROBABILITY, STATISTICS, OR PSYCHIC ABILITY?

Researchers at the website FiveThirtyEight really like playing with numbers, probabilities, and predictions. Consider one researcher, Walt Hickey, who decided to learn more about himself by going to a psychic. First, a psychic reading tarot cards told Hickey (2014) about his dating prospects: He wants someone "stable and confident," but meeting such a person will occur not during the next summer month but possibly in about four months.

Hickey uncovered published psychological research that shows "loyalty" and being "expressive and open" are some of the traits most desired in a potential romantic relationship. He felt these concepts were pretty close to "stable and confident" and that, based on scientific studies, the psychic's declarations of what Hickey wanted in a date had a high probability of being fairly accurate guesses.

In addition, Hickey learned from researchers looking at data on Facebook and the OKCupid dating site that people in New York City (as he is) are more likely to be single and that people on a dating site take a median of 198 days to find a successful match. Perhaps the psychic's estimate of over 120 days was not too far off. Then the psychic told him that many of his friends were going to start getting married. Given that Hickey is 23, this estimate was not too large a stretch, since the median marriage age for college-grad men is almost 30. *Based on probability concepts, how would you interpret what psychics often tell their clients?*

Hickey (2014) concludes:

> Maybe the success of the [psychic] enterprise is based on reminding people of events that could probabilistically transpire. Maybe rather than confirmation bias being an argument against the whole process, it's the thing that makes it work. . . . Even though predicting exactly what's going to happen is hard, we can broadly predict a lot of things about people and the future with a little bit of reading.

And, we would add, critical thinking!

KEY TERMS

COINCIDENCE Two or more events linked by some shared meaning even without a causal connection. Sometimes called *synchronicity*.

CONFIRMATION BIAS OR SUBJECTIVE VALIDATION Ignoring conflicting information and focusing only on those dimensions that reinforce already-held views.

DISJOINT PROBABILITY The likelihood of occurrence of two mutually exclusive events one of which cannot occur at the same time as the other. Add the probabilities.

FORER EFFECT A selective perception process of agreeing with information that sounds positive even when false.

INTERSECTION PROBABILITY The chances of two independent events occurring at the same time. Multiply the probabilities.

LAW OF TRULY LARGE NUMBERS With an increasing number of cases, rare events are more likely to occur.

NULL HYPOTHESIS Untested statement of no difference or no association between groups or measurements.

ODDS Ratio of likelihood of an event occurring divided by the likelihood of that event not occurring.

P VALUE The probability of finding the statistical result by chance when the null hypothesis is true.

PROBABILITY Percentage or fraction calculated by dividing a desired outcome by all possible outcomes.

SELECTIVE PERCEPTION AND RETENTION Seeing and remembering things based on one's frame of reference or biases.

STATISTICAL SIGNIFICANCE Based on the probability of a result occurring by chance, typically at least 0.05 (represented as $p<.05$). If significant, the null hypothesis is rejected.

EXERCISES

1. People post many personal items about coincidences on Facebook. How would you respond to some of these posted comments using your critical thinking tools?

   (a) What are the odds that my best friend from high school would know my husband's best friend from his high school almost 200 miles away from my school?

   (b) While watching a baseball game, I kept thinking that the next batter would hit a home run. Sure enough, he did!

   (c) I had not heard from my cousin in several weeks, and last night I dreamed that she was going to call me. Guess what? She called that morning.

   (d) I registered on several online dating services and was finding absolutely no one of interest. So I decided to quit them. But after

I looked one more time on one of the sites, I saw a new guy whose profile I hadn't seen before. At that very same time, he messaged me and said, "Hi, what's up?" We exchanged phone numbers, and the last three digits were the same for both of us. Not only that: when he sent his first text, it arrived at 3:26. I can't believe it, but 326 is my favorite number of all time, because it was my parents' address when I was growing up!

2. There's a bag filled with 100 jelly beans: 40 are red (cherry), 30 are black (licorice), 24 are yellow (lemon), 5 are blue (blueberry), and 1 is white (coconut). You get to reach into the bag and pick out some candy.

   (a) You get to pick one piece. What is the probability that you will pick out a black (licorice) jelly bean? What are the odds?

   (b) You put the jelly bean back in the bag. What is the probability of picking out two yellow (lemon) candies in a row if you have to put the first one back in the bag?

   (c) What if you get to eat the first yellow one before you get to choose again?

   (d) What's the probability of getting a blue (blueberry) *or* a yellow (lemon) jelly bean?

   (e) Let's say you reach in and get the white (coconut) jelly bean. How is this related to a statistical finding of $p < .01$?

3. Now that you know about probabilities and coincidence, how would you interpret this quotation from the author Vladimir Nabokov's novel *Laughter in the Dark?*

   A certain man once lost a diamond cuff-link in the wide blue sea, and twenty years later, on the exact day, a Friday apparently, he was eating a large fish— but there was no diamond inside. That's what I like about coincidence.

4. You're on a winning streak. You've flipped a coin ten times and have turned up ten heads in a row. Amazing. Now you bet you will flip tails. It has to be. Or so the *gambler's fallacy* (sometimes also called the *Monte Carlo fallacy*) suggests. Using probability concepts, explain why this is called a fallacy and why believing in the concept of a winning streak does not demonstrate critical thinking!

5. Running into someone you know in an unexpected place or talking to someone who knows someone you know well often seems to

characterize what we call "coincidence." Yet, how unusual is it? *Social Network Analysis* (SNA) is a mathematical and visual technique used to study such degrees of separation among groups of people. It considers the paths and connections to others in a network (friendships, workplace, political body, etc.). The centrality of a person, the closeness (the shortest paths) to others, and location between people are all considered in order to determine power and decision-making abilities in a group.

(a) Pick a group of people you hang out with (a friendship group, a floor in a residence hall, a club you belong to, etc.);

(b) draw a set of circles with the names (or just the initials) of the people in the group; and

(c) then connect them to one another with lines indicating who talks to or texts with which others regularly.

(d) What can you conclude about this social network? How does that make you think about probability and coincidence?

CHAPTER 4

Visual Thinking

Critical Thinking, Step Four: How accurately are the illustrations and graphs communicating the results and meanings of the findings? Creating visuals with a minimum use of words is a quick method to convey information effectively. Interpreting data and relationships in graphs is a key critical thinking skill. This chapter presents various ways of visualizing data and presenting results graphically. This chapter also provides tools to critically detect faulty graphics that incorrectly display information or have misleading interpretations, and to construct graphs and charts effectively.

In 2014 the Reuters news agency published a graph seemingly indicating a decline in gun deaths in Florida after that state enacted its controversial "stand your ground" law (Engel, 2014). This law allows individuals to use force to defend themselves without first attempting to retreat when facing a threat. Yet the article described the opposite: an increase in murders.

Turns out, the *y*-axis (vertical scale on the left) went in the wrong direction, with zero at the top instead of in its usual location, at the bottom of the axis, as the line graph in figure 2, using similar data, illustrates. Just as the *x*-axis (horizontal scale at the bottom) goes from an earlier date to a later date, the convention in presenting charts is to have the *y*-axis also go from a lower number to a higher number. Figure 3 is a redo of the chart with the *y*-axis beginning at zero, as is customary. Now it more accurately shows a dramatic increase in gun deaths after 2005, when the law went into effect.

Essential critical thinking tools include learning to evaluate visual presentations of quantitative findings and to create them effectively and honestly. Articles in professional journals and scientific reports typically contain graphics and tables to illustrate the research data, and many readers can find these visual representations confusing.

Presenting accurate visualizations of data is linked to clearly formulating coherent and testable research questions. Sometimes intentionally,

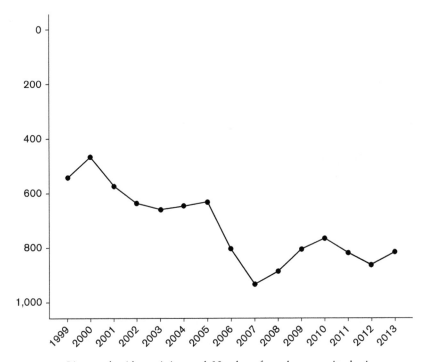

FIGURE 2. Line graph with y-axis inverted: Number of murders committed using guns in Florida, 1999–2013. (Florida Department of Law Enforcement.)

sometimes accidentally, and sometimes inappropriately, graphs and charts are distorted. Data may be too complex for the graph chosen, or someone wishes to communicate a deceptive view, or inexperience leads to poorly designed and incorrect data visualizations.

What makes a good graph or chart? Tufte (2001: 13) provides these basic principles when communicating complex ideas with "clarity, precision, and efficiency." Visualization should:

- show the data;
- induce the viewer to think about the substance rather than about methodology, graphic design, the technology of graphic production, or something else;
- avoid distorting what the data have to say;
- present many numbers in a small space;
- make large data sets coherent;

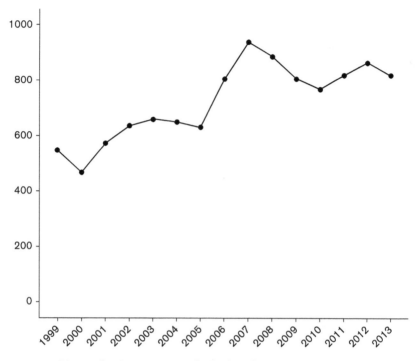

FIGURE 3. Line graph (Figure 2) corrected: Number of murders committed using firearms, 1999–2013. (Florida Department of Law Enforcement.)

- encourage the eye to compare different pieces of data;
- reveal the data at several levels of detail, from a broad overview to the fine structure;
- serve a reasonably clear purpose: description, exploration, tabulation, or decoration;
- be closely integrated with the statistical and verbal descriptions of a data set.

Learning to present data visually and in tables, to read charts, and to interpret graphs is the focus of many critical thinking and quantitative reasoning programs. Take the Maryland State Department of Education, which funded a resource website to aid teachers in designing lesson plans for their elementary and secondary students. Here are the basic questions that it suggests students should ask when interpreting graphic data (MDK12.org, 2016):

- What is the title of the chart, table or graph?
- What is the purpose of this chart, table, or graph?
- What do the labels/headings tell you?
- What key information does the data provide?
- What is your main conclusion about these data?
- How were you able to interpret this chart, table, or graph?

CRITICAL THINKING TIP

When interpreting graphic data, add several more advanced questions: Are the visual representations appropriate for the way the variables are measured? Are the units used in the charts or tables consistent with the data and the purpose of the study? Can you detect any distortions, misused data, or inappropriate choice of graphics? What other visual representations might have been used for these results? Would other choices have resulted in different interpretations of the findings?

SELECTING VISUAL OPTIONS

Choosing the appropriate visual display requires familiarity with both the limitations of some basic graphics and the levels of measurement used to collect the data. Let's review several basic ways of presenting data and in the process introduce examples that distorted the visualization or used an inappropriate graphic.

Bar Charts or Graphs

For a quick visualization of descriptive or comparative information at the nominal or ordinal level of measurement, bar graphs illustrate the distribution of a variable. The nominal categories of a variable are placed along the x-axis (the horizontal scale), and the frequencies (in percentages or raw numbers) of occurrence in the study are located on the y-axis (the vertical scale), when presenting one variable at a time. Bars are created to visually indicate with their height the frequency of occurrence of a value in comparison with the other bars.

Take a look at several graphs and charts using data from the General Social Survey (GSS) and the SPSS data analysis program. The GSS is a

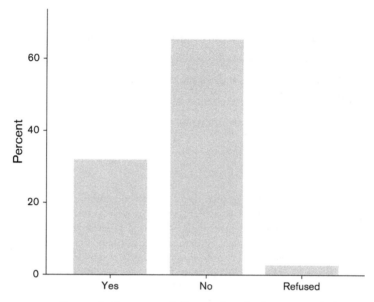

FIGURE 4. Bar graph: Percentage of all respondents having a gun in the home.

highly representative multistage probability sample that has regularly interviewed thousands of U.S. adults (18 and over) since 1972 about their opinions on social issues, behaviors, and demographic characteristics. Since we began with an example related to gun issues, and it's a topic repeatedly argued in the media today, let's continue with that topic from the 2012 and 2014 GSS surveys ($N = 4,512$).

A quick glance at figure 4 tells you right away the most commonly selected category (*yes, no, refuse to answer*) on this GSS question: "Do you happen to have in your home any guns or revolvers?"

You may not be able to specify the exact percentage of respondents who have a gun in their home by looking at the chart in figure 4, but in view of the heights of the bars you can at least see that around twice as many said no than answered yes.

Now look at this survey item: "Are you currently—married, widowed, divorced, separated, or have you never been married?" The category values are placed on the *x*-axis in figure 5, and the frequency percentage on the *y*-axis for the marital status variable.

Keeping in mind some of the questions listed earlier that should guide your critical thinking about visual interpretations, what would you say

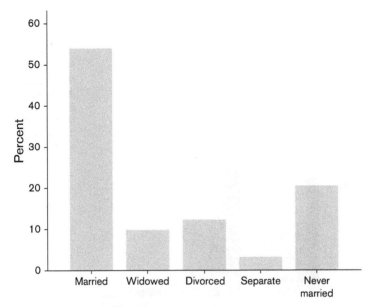

FIGURE 5. Bar graph: Marital status of respondents shown as percentage of all respondents.

these two bar charts tell you about those respondents completing the GSS? Are bar charts an appropriate choice for this level of measurement?

Reading a report with these two charts would provide you some description of the people surveyed and—given the representative sampling—what could be generalized to the U.S. population in those survey years. If the goal is simply to describe the sample on a few items, these charts would suffice. Yet, *what might you consider for another visually informative bar chart with these two descriptive findings?* Critical thinking also involves integrating and applying new information. For example, could gun ownership differ by marital status? Let's combine these variables into one bar graph, figure 6. *What key information does this bar chart provide? What is your main conclusion, and how did you decide this based on your visual interpretation?*

Histograms

When the data are continuous ordinal or interval/ratio measures, another type of bar graph can be used. To illustrate the continuous and

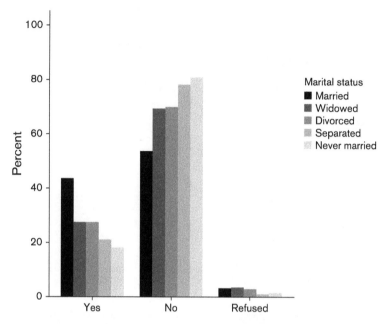

FIGURE 6. Bar graph: Percentage of all respondents having a gun in the home versus marital status of all respondents.

ordered nature of a measure, histograms present the bars as adjacent and contiguous. The amount of area making up each bar's height and width indicates its frequency. Figure 7 depicts the age of respondents participating in the 2012–2014 GSS samples.

These graphs are not appropriate for unordered nominal or discrete categories (like marital status, religion, or place of birth), since the adjacent bars imply continuity between the values. Imposing a normal curve on the chart provides additional visual evidence about the distribution of the variable in the sample and how skewed it may be.

> ### CRITICAL THINKING TIP
>
> Interpreting charts and tables of data requires critically analyzing how the variables are measured, the purpose of the study, the clarity of the images, and the message communicated by the visual. Are these the most appropriate visual presentations?

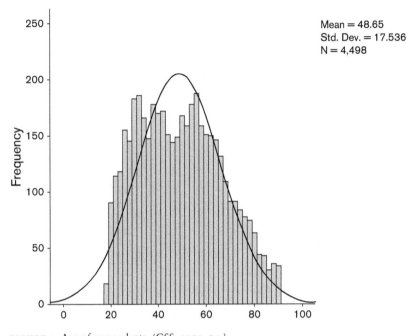

FIGURE 7. Age of respondents. (GSS, 2012–14.)

Altering the Scale

Learning to critically interpret bar charts and histograms also involves carefully evaluating how they are presented. Consider some ways these charts can be distorted. In figure 8, we see what appears visually to be a large difference in response to the 2014 GSS question "Would you favor or oppose a law which would require a person to obtain a police permit before he or she could buy a gun?" The bar is clearly much higher for those respondents who favor a gun permit. However, we cannot really tell how large a difference there is. *What information do you need in order to make better sense of the findings in the survey?*

Before interpreting a graph, it's important first to have evaluated the basic elements of the survey (as discussed in the previous chapters), such as the wording of the items, the levels of measurement, the sampling methods, and response rates. In this case, we know that the wording of items from the General Social Survey (GSS) has been evaluated for validity and reliability and that the GSS uses a representative multistage

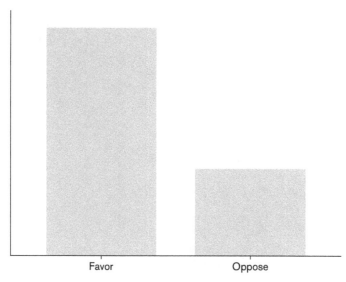

FIGURE 8. Favor or oppose gun permits. (GSS, 2014.)

probability sampling method for its national study. But note that the item asks about police permits. *Would different responses result if the question was worded with the more politically charged phrase "gun control"?*

The item responses are a dichotomy: that is, two nominal categories labeled "favor" or "oppose." Bar charts are therefore a good visual choice in presenting the results. Yet, to complete the picture, the chart should add the number of respondents who answered the question ($N = 1,693$) and show the scale used on the y-axis.

Figure 9 includes a y-axis scale, yet it now looks as if respondents overwhelmingly favor police permits for guns. Note how easy it is to distort the statistical descriptions of the data set (to use Tufte's words from his basic principles listed earlier), especially when there is no report of the actual percentage of respondents choosing "favor" and "oppose." *What problem do you see with this bar chart?*

The actual results show that about 72 percent of respondents favor gun permits, and 28 percent oppose them. Notice what happens in figure 10, when a more accurate range of units is used on the y-axis. Although it is customary to begin bar chart scales with zero, there are situations in which zero is not used as the starting point if the visual distorts the results.

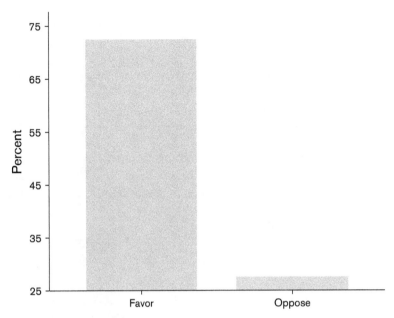

FIGURE 9. Bar graph: Percentage of all respondents who favor or oppose gun permits. (GSS, 2014.)

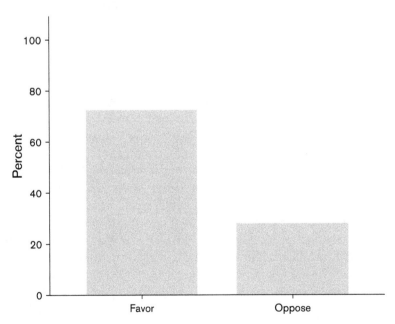

FIGURE 10. Bar graph: Percentage of all respondents who favor or oppose gun permits (N = 1,693).

> **CRITICAL THINKING TIP**
>
> When reading a chart or graph, first check to see what units are used along the horizontal (*x*) and vertical (*y*) axes. Are they reasonable scales, correctly ordered, and relevant to the data being depicted visually?

Remember that when viewing a graph or chart, one's first impression is the visual body, not the numbers or scale used. Critical thinking requires evaluating the entire graph, not just the bars, lines, or pie slices.

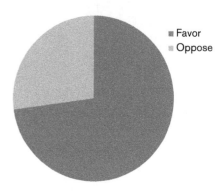

FIGURE 11. Pie chart: Respondents favoring or opposing gun permits.

Pie Charts

Pie charts are an alternative quick visual way of depicting the values of a nominal or categorical variable by using the slices of a circle to indicate size or percentage of each category relative to the others. They are not used very often for more complex data with many categories and are not ideal when looking to compare information. But as a quick visual that can be interpreted without *y*-axis scales, they make a simple and compact visual presentation. Although it may be helpful to indicate the exact percentages of each response or slice of the pie, you know immediately that the total is 100 percent, and the sizes of the slices efficiently indicate their relative proportion without numbers.

Look at figure 11, a pie chart from the same GSS data in response to the same question as was posed above: "Would you favor or oppose a law which would require a person to obtain a police permit before he or she could buy a gun?" Even without knowing the exact per-

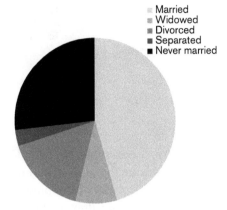

FIGURE 12. Pie chart: Respondents' marital status.

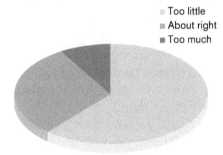

FIGURE 13. 3-D pie chart: Respondents' views on halting a rising crime rate.

centages, you visually obtain an immediate conclusion of favoring gun permits.

However, pie charts are not as visually useful when there are more than a few categories or when depicting two variables together like marital status and gun permits. Compare marital status as a pie chart (fig. 12) with the bar charts shown earlier (figs. 5 and 6).

Which to you is easier to read visually and quickly? Which graph would you choose as more appropriate for these marital status responses?

Altering the Perspective

Even something as simple as a pie chart can be misused to communicate a different outcome. Many statistical programs, such as SPSS, provide alternative ways for displaying graphs, including the use of so-called 3-D views. But these can easily distort information by manipulating the

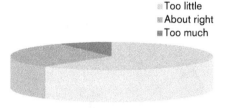

FIGURE 14. 3-D pie chart: Respondents' views on halting a rising crime rate.

angle and area presented in the graphic. Take, for example, the two pie charts shown in figures 13 and 14, which illustrate the same data. Figure 13, the first 3-D chart, seems like a somewhat reasonable representation of the responses to the GSS question "Are we spending too much, too little, or about the right amount on halting the rising crime rate?"

But tilt the angle further, and figure 14, the second 3-D pie chart, using the exact same results, leads to slices that no longer appear representative of the data. The slice at the bottom of an angled pie chart also gets exaggerated simply by its apparent location, closest to the viewer. The area covered by the height of the slice and the angle tend to make the "too little" category seem larger and the "too much" response smaller than they are in figure 13, the first pie chart.

The techniques used to distort figure 14, the second chart, could easily convey inaccurate information about different positions on crime or, say, by an unscrupulous marketing company to illustrate opinions about a client's product. Pie charts are generally not the best method to present data with more than three categories. And when presented with a 3-D version, the critical thinker needs to especially evaluate the information being communicated.

CRITICAL THINKING TIP

When reading a chart or graph, evaluate whether the effects used to make it more exciting with 3-D or other design features are necessary. Are they distorting the data and the interpretation of the findings?

Line Graphs (Frequency Polygons)

A line graph is ideal for visually indicating continuity but not for discrete or categorical data. Let's take the age variable presented in the

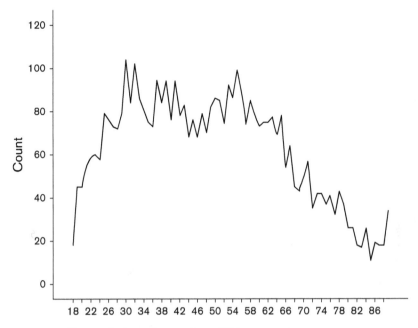

FIGURE 15. Line graph: Ages of respondents. (GSS, 2012–14.)

histogram earlier. Figure 15 shows a line graph version, in essence link-
ing the midpoint of each of the histogram bars with a line. It visually
illustrates the distribution of the age variable in the GSS data set.

Line graphs are especially useful for indicating change in a variable
over time. For example, figure 16, a line graph based on the GSS data
from 2000–2014, at first sight seems to suggest that the mean number
of hours respondents work in a week has fluctuated widely through the
years, especially during the recession from 2008 through 2012. As with
most graphics, the viewer looks quickly at the shape and dimensions of
the illustration and can swiftly draw a conclusion. However, the critical
thinker needs to evaluate all the elements of the chart.

Truncating

As with the bar and pie charts, line graphs are also subject to misuse and
distortions. Figure 16 shows only a portion of the range of units on the
y-axis. Note that in this graph the y-axis ranges from 34 to 40. Truncating the scale is sometimes used to misrepresent the findings. So how
do you determine what numbers to use in line graphs? Occasionally,

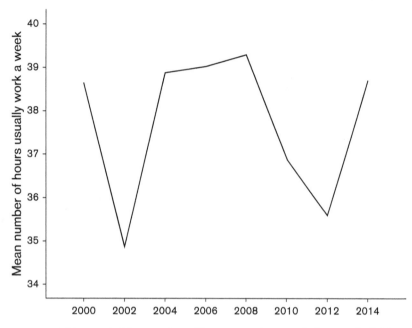

FIGURE 16. Line graph: Mean number of hours respondents worked per week. (GSS, 2014.)

saving space requires presenting smaller graphs, with just a portion of the chart. Also, when representing very small changes over time, such as fluctuations in the stock market, or when it is not possible to have zero as a possible response (such as when illustrating weight or cholesterol levels), it may actually be better not to begin the axis with zero.

CRITICAL THINKING TIP

When reading a chart or graph, think about what it may look like with different units along the axes. Is the size of the visual image appropriate for the research question and the data? Clarity should determine how you accurately communicate the findings and the shape, scale, and size of the visualizations.

Let's alter the scale and instead use zero as the starting point to see how in this case it may result in a distorted visual message. (See figure 17.)

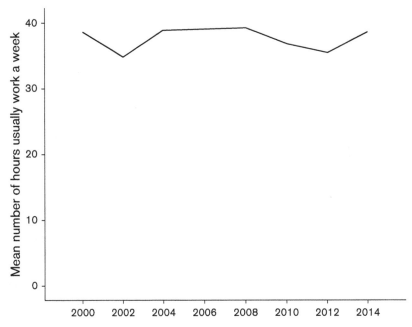

FIGURE 17. Line graph: Mean number of hours respondents worked per week. (GSS, 2014.)

Although a decline can still be seen across the later years, the actual range does not seem so dramatic now. Because of the large blank space below the frequency curve, it's not the best visualization. *Which graph, then, is a more accurate representation of the data?*

Changing the ratio of the height and width of a chart can also subtly affect what is being communicated. Let's take this same line graph and see what it looks like in figure 18, when the width and height of the chart are slightly altered (and not just the *y*-axis scale). Although the line graph may not appear as distorted here, width and height changes may have significant effects on the visual image.

Another way of misrepresenting the data is to modify the highest number on the *y*-axis scale. Figure 19 shows a *y*-axis ranging from zero to 100, not a likely mean number of hours that respondents would work in a week. Notice, though, how the later recession years, from 2008 to 2012, seem less volatile when compared with figure 16, the first line graph used earlier. Choose the scales that best represent the story you want to communicate ethically and accurately about the data.

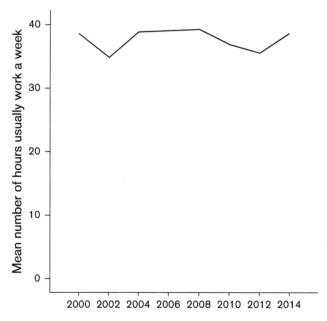

FIGURE 18. Line graph: Mean number of hours respondents worked per week. (GSS, 2014.)

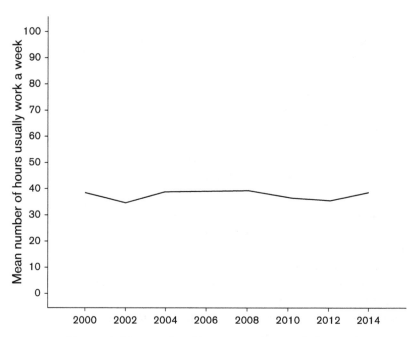

FIGURE 19. Line graph: Mean number of hours respondents worked per week. (GSS, 2014.)

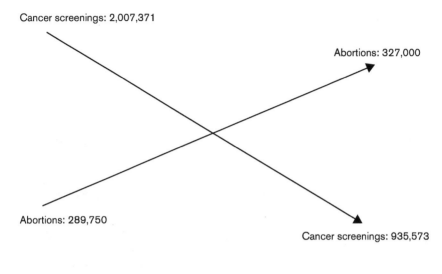

Cancer screenings: 2,007,371

Abortions: 327,000

Abortions: 289,750

Cancer screenings: 935,573

2006   2007   2008   2009   2010   2011   2012   2013

FIGURE 19. Line graph based on Americans United for Life presentation of Planned Parenthood abortions and cancer screenings, 2006–13.

Consider this example from a political campaign by Americans United for Life (2015) against Planned Parenthood and how it distorted data for its purposes at a congressional hearing. Critically review the line graphs shown in figure 19, indicating the number of abortions and the number of cancer screenings performed by Planned Parenthood from 2006 to 2013. *What do you notice about this chart?*

It seems to imply that around 2010 abortions overtook cancer-screening services at Planned Parenthood locations. A scale for the y-axis is obviously missing. See what happens in figure 20, when a scale of 600,000 intervals is added in order to capture the wide range of data presented in Planned Parenthood's annual reports.

Note that there is no point where the number of abortions exceeds cancer services. Tests for cancer have declined as a result of recommendations for less frequent Pap smears to test for women's cervical cancer, more opportunities to be screened for cancer elsewhere without cost as a result of the Affordable Care Act, and in part because of the closing of Planned Parenthood clinics (Qiu, 2015).

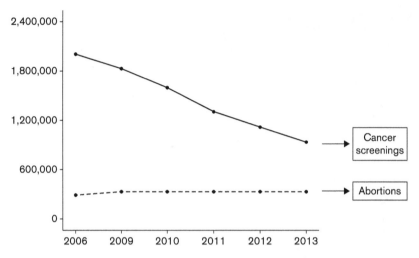

FIGURE 21. Line graph based on Planned Parenthood abortions and cancer screenings, 2006–13.

Tables: Crosstabs

In many situations, a table can be an effective visualization method for presenting data, certainly more effective than a poorly constructed or distorted chart or graph. Many times readers prefer seeing the actual numbers and not just the relative sizes of pie slices or bars. Learning to interpret tables of data and to construct relevant ones is central to developing critical thinking skills.

Cross-tabulations, sometimes called *contingency tables,* are a common way to depict a summary relationship between two categorical or ordered discrete variables. The outcome variable is contingent or dependent on the possible causal or independent variable. In order to interpret cross-tabulations (crosstabs), it's important to learn which are the rows and which the columns. As in any spreadsheet, rows typically go across horizontally (like seats in a theater) and contain the values of the outcome (or dependent) variable. The columns are vertical (like those holding up a classical Greek temple's roof) and usually represent the values of the independent (or causal) variable. The point where a row and a column meet in a table is called a *cell.* Tables are often described in terms of the number of rows by the number of columns, as with table 4, a 3-by-4 table (with 12 cells).

Table 4, an SPSS table using the GSS data, represents a relationship between how much education respondents (N = 5,917) have achieved

TABLE 4 CROSS-TABULATION: CONFIDENCE IN CONGRESS AND EDUCATIONAL LEVEL

| | | Highest Education | | | | | |
		Less than High School	High School	Junior College	Bachelor	Graduate	Total
Confidence in Congress	A great deal						
	Count	133	255	48	81	30	547
	% within highest education	15.2%	8.9%	9.8%	7.5%	5.1%	9.2%
	Only some						
	Count	427	1422	248	511	307	2915
	% within highest education	48.9%	49.4%	50.5%	47.1%	52.0%	49.3%
	Hardly any						
	Count	313	1200	195	494	253	2455
	% within highest education	35.9%	41.7%	39.7%	45.5%	42.9%	41.5%
Total	Count	873	2877	491	1086	590	5917
	% within highest education	100.0%	100.0%	100.0%	100.0%	100.0%	100.0%

and how much confidence they have in the U.S. Congress. Since we are assuming that their opinions are contingent on their education (after all, holding an opinion on Congress doesn't normally lead to earning degrees), educational degrees are placed in the columns and confidence measures in the rows.

We can read table 4 as follows (for example, row 1, column 4): 81 respondents with bachelor's degrees have a great deal of confidence in Congress (that's 7.5% of all 1,086 respondents with only a college degree). Compare this with 133 respondents (15.2% in row 1, column 1) who have less than a high school diploma and hold a great deal of confidence in Congress. In terms of percentage, 15.2 percent is twice as many as those with a college degree. You can't compare just the frequency count, since there are 873 respondents with the lowest educational level and 1,086 with a college degree. As discussed in chapter 1, percentages standardize the counts and allow you to make comparisons across columns with unequal numbers.

What is often confusing is in which direction to calculate the percentages. Remember that each category of the independent (or causal) variable must add up to 100 percent, regardless of whether that variable is in the row or the column. However, it is customary to place the independent variables in the columns. Knowing these guidelines also means tables can be misused.

Confusing Rows and Columns in Tables

Imagine you reversed the percentages and made each dependent variable category (confidence level in Congress) in the rows add up to 100 percent. You would get table 5, where 81 respondents with a bachelor's degree, for example, still have a great deal of confidence in Congress, as in table 4. *How would you read this number and percentage?* Note that 81 is now 14.8 percent of all 547 respondents having a great deal of confidence in Congress—a very different result. In table 5, you can only compare across rows to answer another question, What percentage of each level of confidence is made up of various educational attainments?

That's not the same as asking what percentage of people at each level of education holds various opinions about Congress. To put it another way, imagine you did a survey of psychology majors on campus. You could ask what percentage of those majors are women, or you could ask what percentage of women are psych majors: two different questions

TABLE 5   CROSS-TABULATION: CONFIDENCE IN CONGRESS AND RESPONDENT'S EDUCATIONAL LEVEL

		Highest Education					
		Less than High School	High School	Junior College	Bachelor	Graduate	Total
Confidence in Congress	A great deal	Count					
		133	255	48	81	30	547
		% within confidence	24.3%	46.6%	8.8%	14.8%	5.5%	100.0%
	Only some	Count					
		427	1422	248	511	307	2915
		% within confidence	14.6%	48.8%	8.5%	17.5%	10.5%	100.0%
	Hardly any	Count					
		313	1200	195	494	253	2455
		% within confidence	12.7%	48.9%	7.9%	20.1%	10.3%	100.0%
Total		Count					
		873	2877	491	1086	590	5917
		% within confidence	14.8%	48.6%	8.3%	18.4%	10.0%	100.0%

requiring two different presentations in a crosstab. Did you discover that 80 percent of psychology majors are women, or that 80 percent of women are psychology majors? Critical thinking is essential when formulating the appropriate research question and required when illustrating your findings in table form.

CRITICAL THINKING TIP

When reading contingency tables (or crosstabs), check to see whether the independent variable is in the columns and if each column totals 100 percent. Take any cell and verbally read it aloud in terms of the variables, such as: X percent of respondents who selected the column variable category also chose the row variable category (for example, 20 percent of juniors declared a sociology major). Is that correctly illustrating the topic of the table and the research question?

OTHER GRAPHICS

There are many other kinds of charts, graphs, and creative visualizations, thanks to the sophistication of computer software and designers. Most of the critical thinking tips apply also to any visual depiction of data. Are the units appropriate for the data and level of measurement? Are the images used relevant to the research goals? Do alternative ways to illustrate the findings change the interpretations and meanings?

In the classic book *How to Lie with Statistics,* Darrell Huff (1954) pointed out how some maps distort information by not distinguishing between area size and population size. These two different perspectives are best illustrated in U.S. presidential election results. The media typically present popular votes in states, using red (in fig. 22, light gray) for the Republican candidate and blue (dark gray in fig. 22) for the Democratic candidate.

Immediately, the visualization suggests that the winner *of the popular vote* in this 2016 map is the Republican candidate, Donald Trump, given all the gray in the 48 continental states. However, we know that the popular vote results were very close and that the Democratic candidate, Hillary Clinton, received almost three million more votes. So why isn't dark gray at least equal to or greater than the dominant color? As Huff pointed out, land area is not the same as population area. The

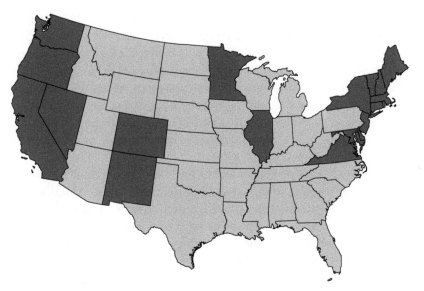

FIGURE 22. U.S. presidential election, 2016: votes based on population (light gray for Republican candidate, dark gray for Democratic candidate). (From Newman, 2016.)

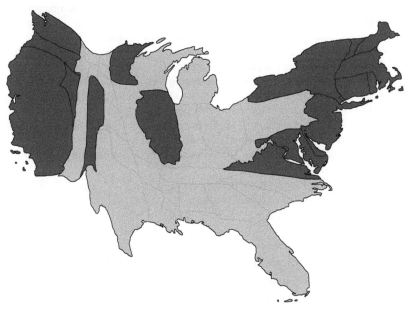

FIGURE 23. U.S. presidential election, 2016: votes based on land size of states (light gray for Republican candidate, dark gray for Democratic candidate). (From Newman, 2016. http://www-personal.umich.edu/~mejn/election/2012/faq.html.)

dark gray states represent much higher populations, and the light gray states tend to have lower populations, on average.

Newman (2016) recreated the map as in figure 23, so that "the sizes of states are rescaled according to their population. That is, states are drawn with size proportional not to their acreage but to the number of their inhabitants, states with more people appearing larger than states with fewer, regardless of their actual area on the ground." Now the colors visually reflect more accurately the closeness of the popular vote.

As with all types of graphs and charts, illustrations must follow the goals of the project; communicate information clearly, ethically, and efficiently; and provide appropriate connection between how the variables are measured and the graphics selected. Critical thinking involves evaluating these elements and uncovering any distortions and misuse of the basic standards of each type of chart or graph.

KEY TERMS

BAR CHART A chart employing rectangles to depict the proportion of responses for each value of a nominal or ordinal variable.

CROSSTAB (OR CONTINGENCY TABLE) A table depicting the relationship between two nominal or ordinal variables in rows (dependent or outcome variables) and columns (independent or causal variables).

HISTOGRAM A bar chart employing contiguous rectangles to indicate the frequency of values for interval/ratio variables.

LINE GRAPH A series of points representing values of a continuous variable interconnected with a line, sometimes (when it joins the midpoints of the tops of the histogram bars) called a *frequency polygon*.

PIE CHART A circular chart in which the slices represent the relative proportions of the values of a nominal or ordinal variable.

TRUNCATION A common way to distort a graph, truncating the scale on the chart's y-axis.

X-AXIS Horizontal scale on a graph or chart.

Y-AXIS Vertical scale on a graph or chart.

EXERCISES

1. Figure 24 is a line graph, but something is just not right. The goal is to illustrate how many people of different races completed the survey. Describe the major problem with the chart and suggest what should be done instead to depict visually the distribution of races in the study more accurately.

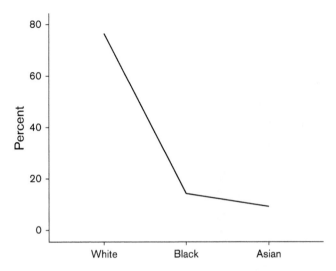

FIGURE 24. Line graph: Race of respondents as percentage of respondents. (GSS, 2014.)

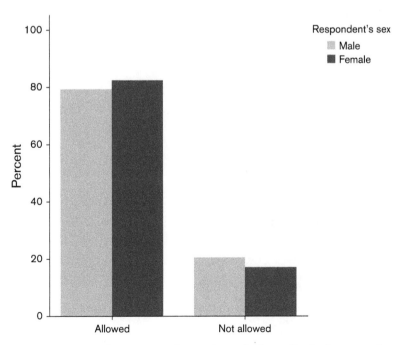

FIGURE 25. Bar graph: Percentage of respondents who favor allowing homosexuals to teach, male versus female.

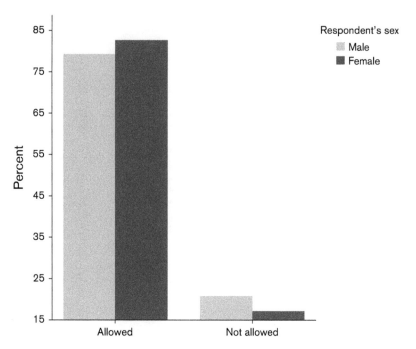

FIGURE 26. Bar graph: Percentage of respondents who favor allowing homosexuals to teach, male versus female.

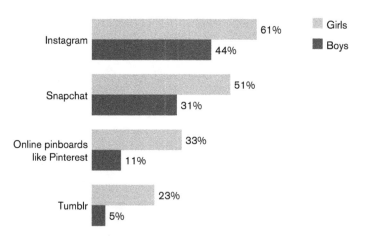

FIGURE 27. Bar graph: Percentage of respondents using four social media sites, boys versus girls.

2. Figure 25's bar graph combines two variables from the General Social Survey: sex of respondent and the respondents' opinions about allowing gay people to teach in schools.
   (a) Put into words what this chart is communicating.
   (b) What could be a problem if it were presented instead as in figure 26?

3. The Pew Research Center (2015d) conducted a survey of teenagers' (13–17 years old) use of social media. Figure 27 shows the results, presented as a bar chart of the percentage of boys and of girls using different platforms:
   (a) Put into words what this bar chart is describing.
   (b) Create a cross-tabulation with these data. *Hint:* The numbers for those teens who don't use those particular social media are omitted from the bar chart.

CHAPTER 5

Correlation and Causation

Critical Thinking, Step 5: What is required to conclude that there is a cause-and-effect relationship in the research that you are encountering? Associations between two or more variables can be statistically meaningful; yet assuming that some cause the others requires several other important conditions. What are the elements necessary for a causal relationship and the methods used to eliminate alternative explanations? This chapter provides the critical thinking tools to assess the accuracy of media reports of research studies that seem to suggest cause-and-effect results.

Believe it or not, the following statement is strongly supported by statistical analysis: There's an almost perfect correlation ($r = 0.96$) in the United States between per capita consumption of mozzarella cheese and the number of civil engineering doctorates awarded in a ten-year period!

According to these data (Vigen, 2015), as shown in table 6, when people consumed more of this cheese, more Ph.D.s were earned in civil engineering. Really. The message is pretty clear—eating mozzarella results in getting an engineering Ph.D. Let's run out and order some extra-cheese pizzas instead of studying for our degrees.

Humorous as this silly example may be, it illustrates a serious and common critical thinking error—*confusing correlation with causation*—that could create much misunderstanding and lead to problematic public policy and unethical personal decisions.

DEFINITIONS

Correlation is a statistical concept that mathematically measures the strength of a relationship between at least two variables. As one variable changes at the same rate as another variable, we may be able to conclude there is a co-relation between them. The closer the correlation coefficient is to 1.0, the stronger it is; the closer it is to 0, the weaker it

TABLE 6 CORRELATION BETWEEN CHEESE CONSUMPTION AND CIVIL ENGINEERING
DOCTORATES, 2000–2009

Category	2000	2001	2002	2003	2004	2005	2006	2007	2008	2009
Per capita consumption of mozzarella cheese (U.S.) (pounds)[a]	9.3	9.7	9.7	9.7	9.9	10.2	10.5	11	10.6	10.6
Civil engineering doctorates awarded (U.S.)[b]	480	501	540	552	547	622	655	701	712	708

SOURCE: Vigen, 2015.

[a] Figures from U.S. Department of Agriculture.

[b] Figures from National Science Foundation.

is (or nonexistent). If they vary in opposite directions (that is, as one variable increases, the other one decreases), we would see a negative sign attached to the correlation. Don't be confused: A negative sign does not indicate a weak correlation; it is about direction, not magnitude.

Causation implies that one of the variables is the explanation and source of the variation in the other variable. The independent variable is the cause (X); the dependent variable (Y) is the outcome or effect. Causality can be *probabilistic*—that is, estimates are given about the likelihood of something occurring as the result of a cause rather than any guarantee that it will happen 100 percent of the time. For example, the odds of getting lung cancer (Y) are increased in association with heavy smoking (X). Epidemiologists can specify what the increased probability is for different levels of smoking.

Probabilistic causes can differ from *necessary* causes, which state that in order for Y to happen, X *must* be present. You won't be able to get your degree (Y) if you fail to complete your thesis (X). Writing a thesis is necessary for graduating with a degree. However, it is not *sufficient*, since besides the thesis you must also finish all other course work with passing grades. *What other examples from your own experiences can you give to distinguish probabilistic, necessary, and sufficient causes?*

For any of these types of causality, several conditions must be present to declare causation:

- a strong statistically significant correlation must exist between the two variables;

- the association must be testable, consistent, and substantive;
- the possible cause variable (the independent variable, indicated as X) must occur prior in time to the possible effect variable (the dependent or outcome variable, indicated as Y);
- alternative causes or explanations must be eliminated.

When all these conditions are met, we can conclude with confidence that the correlation demonstrates a greater probability of a cause-and-effect relationship. Let's look more closely at these ideas.

STATISTICAL CORRELATION

We say that things are *correlated* when there is an association or connection between two observations or measurements. Every day we reach conclusions, often without any mathematical evidence, about connections. We don't need statistics to demonstrate that when we eat a big meal we no longer feel hungry. Or when we eat a piece of chocolate we occasionally break out into hives and sneeze because we may be allergic to chocolate. Yet, to realize an association between two phenomena or variables does not necessarily mean that one of them is the cause of the other, the outcome.

Basing public policy on merely anecdotal connections or making life-or-death decisions on such a basis does not demonstrate sophisticated critical thinking skills or scientific reasoning. We must be able to provide systematic evidence that goes beyond our hunches, claims, and intuitions.

Introductory statistics books focus on many possible ways of calculating correlations and associations mathematically. Depending on how the variables are measured or observed, Pearson r, chi-square, Spearman's rho, Analysis of Variance (ANOVA), and t-tests could all be used to establish relationships between variables. Some, like Pearson r, t-tests, and ANOVA, make use of means and therefore require interval/ratio levels of measurement. Spearman's rho is suitable for ordinal measures, and chi-squares can be used with nominal and ordinal data. Each of the statistical calculations that result is then compared with what is expected to occur by chance, and those that occur less than 5 percent of the time (sometimes 1 percent or less) by chance are considered *statistically significant*. This is the first step in deciding whether one variable is the cause of the other. (See chapter 3 for a discussion of statistical probability.)

CRITICAL THINKING TIP

Be sure that there is a meaningful and statistically significant relationship among the variables being evaluated. Causation is not possible when there is a weak correlation or none at all.

Consider this example from the General Social Survey (GSS), which provides annual data on a wide range of issues using a national random sample. Data analysis demonstrates a 0.13 correlation (Pearson r) between age of first marriage and the highest number of years of school completed. Among a group of 1,160 respondents between 2006 and 2012, those who completed more years of education tended to marry at later ages. Although the correlation is small, it is statistically significant. We can state that there is an association between these two variables. This is the first step in deciding a cause-and-effect relationship.

TESTABLE, REPLICATED, AND SUBSTANTIVE

Yet, we are not prepared to conclude causality. Hypothesized relationships must be testable, be demonstrated consistently across other samples, and reflect important findings (unlike cheese consumption and engineering degrees!).

Too often, people propose relationships that are incapable of being tested. Hypotheses must be statements about a possible relationship between variables that can be measured or observed. Correlations between two variables can differ among studies simply because of different types of measurement or how a question is worded. If you wish to explain the mysterious crop circles showing up in farm areas by suggesting visitors from another planet, you should be prepared to provide a good observation tool to record when these ETs arrive. Or if you want to know why a couple broke up their relationship and you hypothesize a change in their love for one another, you need to be able to measure love. These measures must demonstrate *validity*—that is, it must be confirmed that they are measuring what they claim to be measuring. Is your love scale accurately assessing this thing called love?

The simple fact that a statistically significant correlation occurs in one study doesn't provide sufficient evidence to refrain from further assessment. Will a similar relationship also be significant for other samples of respondents? in other locales? or among different ethnicities, genders, and sexual orientations? The association must be *replicated* before we go jumping to any final conclusions. Consider how many times you have heard that drinking coffee is good for you; then another study reports that coffee is not healthy to drink or that red wine is good for the heart— but that is true only if you are a lab rat and drink 100 liters per day. Consistency through replication is required before texting the findings to your friends and posting your Instagram photos of wine and coffee. A research project's measurements must demonstrate some *reliability:* that is, on repeated assessments, the results should be consistent.

Ultimately, there is no point in making conclusions about causality if the findings are not particularly important. Be aware that sometimes small correlation coefficients can artificially have statistical significance because of large sample sizes. This is an issue faced by researchers using so-called Big Data—very large sets of information analyzed with sophisticated computer programs looking for meaningful relationships. With the GSS example between age of first marriage and the highest number of years of school completed, a 0.13 is significant mathematically for a large sample over 1,100 respondents, but that's still a relatively small correlation. *Would a correlation of that size be substantive enough to announce publicly that you uncovered a major finding or be enough to alter some social policy or confidently make a personal decision to proceed with some medical treatment?*

Remember: the closer to 1.0, the stronger the relationship is. A quick rule of thumb is that squaring the correlation (r^2 is 0.13 × 0.13 = 0.017) can indicate what percentage of the outcome (dependent) variable is explained by the independent (perhaps the causal) variable. In this example, number of years of schooling explains 1.7 percent of the reasons why respondents in the sample varied in the ages of first marriage. You can see that it takes a correlation over 0.70 to account for an independent variable explaining at least half of the variation in any outcome variable by squaring 0.70 to get 0.49 (or 49 percent).

CRITICAL THINKING TIP

Ask how reliable and valid the measures and scales in a study are. Is the association among the variables important, meaningful, and strong enough that a cause-and-effect relationship is probable?

Importance is always relative; what is important depends on prior research, interest in the topic, and the politics behind a particular study. You may think a relationship between mozzarella cheese and civil engineering degrees is trivial—unless you work for a cheese company.

So, once you first establish some statistically significant relationship, go on to ask if the variables are testable and capable of being measured accurately (validity), can be consistently replicated (reliability), and are meaningful enough (in terms both of strength of the relationship and importance of the findings). This is the second step in deciding whether there is a causal relationship.

TIMELINE

Let's return to our humorous example about cheese and engineering degrees. A correlation coefficient of 0.96 is extremely impressive. Yet it is difficult to determine whether eating that cheese precedes getting a civil engineering doctorate. Maybe degree recipients celebrated by eating lots of mozzarella pizzas. Or working toward a doctorate involved long evenings of study requiring cheesy food. It goes without saying that a key element in determining cause and effect is verifying that the cause happens before the effect (i.e., that X precedes Y). Sometimes this is easily discovered, as for example when one variable is collected or observed hours, days, or years before another variable is measured. A *longitudinal* study can be a more valid and reliable method for establishing a before-or-after timeline than a *cross-sectional* one, which collects data at a single point in time. For example, you assess mathematical abilities at the start of a class and weeks later, when the course ends, you measure them again to see whether new teaching methods had any impact.

In other cases, especially when cross-sectional methods are used, it is more difficult to determine a time sequence. Do people taking vitamins become healthier, or do healthier people tend to take more vitamins? Does grade-point average occur before or after the number of hours of study per week? Perhaps a high GPA causes people to study more in order to maintain their grades, rather than the other way around. Critically reviewing research designs, looking for comparisons with other similar studies, seeking replication of findings, and invoking simple logic all help to determine a timeline.

Remember that establishing a sequential order is just one element in concluding a cause-and-effect relationship. Basing causality solely on a timeline sequence is a lapse in critical thinking, just as much as is basing causality solely on a significant correlation. There's a Latin expression, often referred to as the *post-hoc fallacy*, which captures this logical error: *post hoc, ergo propter hoc* ("after this, therefore because of this"), or when there is an unknown timeline and the variables appear to occur simultaneously, *cum hoc, ergo propter hoc* ("with this, therefore because of this").

CRITICAL THINKING TIP

Determine the sequence of the variables being evaluated for causality. Is there confidence that the independent measure occurs in time before the dependent variable? Ask what the information may look like if the timeline is reversed.

The mere fact that an outcome variable occurs after or with another variable does not automatically indicate causality. A sequence of events to suggest causality characterizes many superstitions and conspiracy theories, not to mention beliefs in questionable health-related studies. Remember the discussion in chapter 3 on probability and coincidence? *The Skeptic's Dictionary* (Carroll, 2003) provides several good examples of the *post hoc, ergo propter hoc* fallacy:

> You have a cold, so you drink fluids and two weeks later your cold goes away. You have a headache so you stand on your head and six hours later your headache goes away. . . . You use your dowsing stick and then you find water. You imagine heads coming up on a coin toss and heads comes up. You rub your lucky charm and what you wish for comes true. You lose your lucky charm and you strike out six times. You have a "vision" that a body is going to be found near water or in a field and later a body is found near water or in a field.

Can you come up with some everyday examples from your own experience that illustrate this post hoc, ergo propter hoc *fallacy?*

ALTERNATIVE EXPLANATIONS

Presumably, vitamins are an important component of good health. We know that certain vitamins can prevent serious problems and may even serve as a protective barrier against many cancers. Certainly in many of the world's poverty areas lacking nutritious food, a rise in such conditions as scurvy, rickets, and diabetes may be attributed to vitamin deficiencies (of vitamins C, D, and E, for example). It follows, then, that taking daily vitamin supplements (independent variables) should lead to fewer incidences of cancer, diabetes, and other illnesses (dependent variables). In other words, a cause-and-effect relationship may exist between these variables.

But does it, even in developed countries where nutrition, medical care, and healthy lifestyles are more readily available, especially among people who can afford supplemental vitamins? In randomized longitudinal studies carried out by the Women's Health Initiative and the Physicians' Health Study in the United States, no significant differences in cancer, heart disease, mortality rates, or diabetes were evident in those people who took vitamin supplements (primarily C, D, and E) as opposed to those people who did not (Oster, 2014). So why did other studies suggest that taking vitamins makes a difference? Many of those other studies did not depend on randomized samples and did not take into account alternative explanations, as for example education and race. It turns out that less education and not being white were related to more health problems like diabetes and obesity, and to taking fewer vitamin supplements.

So, in the best studies, no significant relationships existed between health and taking vitamin supplements; other variables (race and education) were related to both of those independent and dependent variables. Maybe it's the lifestyles of better-educated people that lead to better health and to taking more vitamins. *Which, then, are the causes, and which are the effects?*

Not every effect has a single cause. Why did you come down with a cold? Not sleeping well, eating poorly, stressing over work to be finished, and failing to wash your hands regularly during flu season are all possible causes that can lead to a cold. And what sometimes can be a cause for a cold in itself can be seen as an outcome in another chain of events. Not sleeping well may be a contributing cause of a cold, but not sleeping well could also be an effect of stressing over unfinished work. There is nothing inherent in a variable that makes it automatically a cause or an effect.

The trick is to figure out which are the most plausible causes in understanding any particular outcome. Just remember that many of these variables can occur simultaneously and can have an impact on one another. It's also important to understand that complex social behaviors or opinions rarely are caused by a single variable and often require a set of interacting causes.

Did you ever see a Rube Goldberg chain of events, where the ultimate endpoint, to take one example, is a bunch of dominoes falling over? This result is dependent on a series of interactive and rigidly sequential causes, no one of which on its own can cause the dominoes to fall. (OK: go ahead; take a break, and search for the Rube Goldberg machine videos!) In many ways, this is an apt metaphor for social behavior. No one cause is likely to explain all the reasons an outcome occurs, since the most proximate cause is itself often an outcome of other variables. Critical thinking involves determining what the other plausible alternative causes may be and figuring out how these variables may or may not contribute to the effect.

An apple a day keeps the doctor away has been a familiar English aphorism in various forms since 1866. It's not just a reminder to eat your daily fruit; perhaps it's also a hint that an apple may work wonders in preventing illnesses serious enough to see a medical expert. Implicit in this sentence is a cause (a daily apple) resulting in an effect (good health). However, may there be other causes of good health that better explain less need to visit a doctor?

A 2015 study (Davis, Bynum, and Sirovich, 2015) found that 39 percent of daily apple eaters did not visit a doctor in the previous year, compared with 34 percent of non–apple eaters; although small, this 5 percent difference is statistically significant. However, apple eaters were also better educated and were less likely to smoke. *Could these explain the better health?* Sure enough, when the study controlled for such differences, the correlation did not persist. So despite a significant relationship of a testable and substantive idea, and a timeline in which eating apples preceded visiting a doctor, we could not declare causation, since plausible alternative explanations washed away any meaningful findings.

Controlling for additional explanatory variables (the causes) is a common and important statistical procedure in research. What was just demonstrated is called a *spurious relationship* when the independent (cause) and dependent (effect) variables are both related to a third (control) variable. The original significant relationship disappears or is no longer statistically significant when this *control variable* is introduced into the analysis.

TABLE 7 CROSS-TABULATION: FATHER'S EDUCATION AND RESPONDENT'S OPINION ON THE DEATH PENALTY, 2012–14

			Father's Education		
			Less than college	College degree or higher	Total
Favor or oppose death penalty for murder	Favor	Count	3637	813	4450
		% within Education	68.5%	63.6%	67.5%
	Oppose	Count	1675	465	2140
		% within Education	31.5%	36.4%	32.5%
Total		Count	5312	1278	6590
		% within Education	100.0%	100.0%	100.0%

CRITICAL THINKING TIP

When reviewing potential cause-and-effect relationships, think about other possible explanations for the outcome variable. What else may explain the relationship? Have the researchers taken into account these alternative variables and controlled for them through their research design or statistical analysis?

Table 7 shows an example from the GSS, with a random sample of 6,590 Americans. There is a significant relationship between the highest degree earned by respondents' fathers and respondents' own opinions on the death penalty (based on chi-square statistic, $p<.001$). Although most respondents favored the death penalty, those respondents whose fathers earned a college degree or higher degree were more opposed than those fathers with less than a college degree (by almost 5%: that is, 36.4% versus 31.5%). *Can we thus conclude that having a more educated father will cause you to oppose the death penalty?*

Fathers' education usually precedes their children's opinions in time, and there is a significant relationship, albeit not a particularly strong one. So that condition is met. But we still need to rule out other possible reasons for this apparent connection before we declare a cause. Given that people's educational attainment is related to parents' educational levels, we may want to see if the respondents' own educations are really what may be influencing their opinions on the death penalty, and not so much their fathers' educational attainment.

So controlling for an alternative explanation, we now see in table 8 that for those respondents with less than a college education, differences in opposing the death penalty are now reduced by 1 percent between those with better-educated fathers and those with less-educated fathers (29.6% versus 28.6%), and by around 3 percent for those respondents with college degrees or higher (37.9% versus 40.8%). Statistical significance levels (based on chi-squares) are $p > .05$, verifying the null hypothesis of no relationship between fathers' education and respondents' opinions on the death penalty when controlling for respondents' own educational attainment.

At other times, alternative variables could show that they are *suppressing* a relationship between an independent and a dependent variable, a relationship that initially appears not to be statistically significant. These possibly causal variables are interrelated themselves (like parents' education and respondents' education) and accordingly the explanatory power of any one of them is minimized. Sometimes, the alternative variables clarify the first relationship with specific conditions: for example, the correlation holds up only for college graduates in the study but not for those respondents with less than a college degree. In any such case, a control variable is used to modify the original relationship and thus eliminate a simple cause-and-effect connection. In short, before any causal explanation can be claimed or refuted, you must critically evaluate and control for plausible alternative variables.

- An *intervening variable* (Z) comes between the independent (X) and dependent (Y) variables and suppresses or elaborates the original relationship: X–Z–Y.
- An *antecedent variable* elaborates the original relationship between X and Y by indicating that X is itself the result of another cause (Z), which may come before the independent variable: Z–X–Y.
- A *spurious relationship* is said to occur when an antecedent variable (Z) related to both X and Y leads to the disappearance of the original correlation between X and Y. What seemed like a relationship no longer exists: Z–X, Z–Y.

TABLE 8 CROSS-TABULATIONS: FATHER'S EDUCATION AND RESPONDENT'S OPINION ABOUT THE DEATH PENALTY, CONTROLLING FFOR RESPONDENT'S EDUCATION, 2012–14

Respondent's education				Father's education		
				Less than college	College degree or higher	Total
Less than college	Favor or oppose death penalty for murder	FAVOR	Count	2857	332	3189
			% within father's education	70.4%	71.4%	70.5%
		OPPOSE	Count	1199	133	1332
			% within father's education	29.6%	28.6%	29.5%
	Total		Count	4056	465	4521
			% within father's education	100.0%	100.0%	100.0%
College degree or higher	Favor or oppose death penalty for murder	FAVOR	Count	779	481	1260
			% within father's education	62.1%	59.2%	60.9%
		OPPOSE	Count	476	332	808
			% within father's education	37.9%	40.8%	39.1%
	Total		Count	1255	813	2068
			% within father's education	100.0%	100.0%	100.0%
Total	Favor or oppose death penalty for murder	FAVOR	Count	3636	813	4449
			% within father's education	68.5%	63.6%	67.5%
		OPPOSE	Count	1675	465	2140
			% within father's education	31.5%	36.4%	32.5%
	Total		Count	5311	1278	6589
			% within father's education	100.0%	100.0%	100.0%

Determining causality is typically the goal of many scientific studies. Epidemiologists, medical researchers, social scientists, and historians all seek ways of uncovering the reasons why something occurs. Why do people vote for different candidates, hold a variety of opinions on gun control, seek reasons for failing health, and fall for urban legends and Internet scams? When reading or hearing studies attempting to answer such questions, critically assess any attempts to claim causality. Implying a cause-and-effect relationship is a very common error in today's media-dominated culture.

KEY TERMS

ALTERNATIVE EXPLANATIONS (CONTROL VARIABLES) Plausible variables that may modify, eliminate, or elaborate an original relationship between independent and dependent variables.

CAUSATION A relationship determined by finding a statistically significant correlation, establishing a timeline between the variables, and controlling for alternative explanations.

CORRELATION COEFFICIENT A mathematical calculation between 0 and (plus or minus) 1 that establishes the strength of a relationship between two variables.

CROSS-SECTIONAL STUDY A study that collects data or observations at one point in time.

LONGITUDINAL STUDY A study that collects data or observations over a specified period of time.

POST HOC, ERGO PROPTER HOC FALLACY Literally, "After this, therefore because of this": A logical fallacy attributing causality to a variable simply on the basis of its having occurred first.

RELIABILITY Consistency across repeated measurements.

SPURIOUS RELATIONSHIP A relationship among variables in which independent and dependent variables appear to be related because each of them is correlated with an alternative variable.

STATISTICAL SIGNIFICANCE Condition said to exist when the probability of obtaining a relationship by chance between two variables is less than a specified number, usually $p<.05$.

TIMELINE A key element necessarily verified in determining causality: an independent variable (cause) must occur before the dependent variable (effect).

VALIDITY Accuracy of measuring what is supposed to be measured.

EXERCISES

1. A classic example: the more fire engines on the scene of a fire, the more damage to the buildings. So, do fire engines cause more damage? Discuss what is being claimed here: How would you go

FIGURE 28. Comic by Randall Munroe. (https://xkcd.com/552/. http://xkcd.com/license.html.)

about refuting (or supporting) this causal claim. How is this related to spurious relationships?

2. A study (Bao et al., 2013) in the *New England Journal of Medicine* reported that eating more nuts was associated with lower risks of mortality. What do you need to do before you can conclude a cause-and-effect relationship? What do you think may make for plausible alternative explanations? Finally, read the article (http://www.nejm.org/doi/full/10.1056/NEJMoa1307352) and evaluate the study and its findings.

3. A controversial social issue today debates the role that childhood vaccinations play in the development of autism. Some claim a cause-and-effect relation; others claim that alternative explanations disprove the relationship between vaccines and autism. Find some articles and create a list of variables used by people who argue the various positions. How would you go about evaluating the information you find? How do the popular media differ from the scientific publications and from parents involved in making decisions?

4. Consider the cartoon in fig. 28. Laugh. Then interpret it for someone who doesn't get it!

CHAPTER 6

Scientific Thinking

Critical Thinking, Step Six: What makes a study scientific, and how does that differ from pseudoscience? Assess research findings and media claims by asking: Is this a study based on anecdotes, or on a more rigorous research design? Are hypotheses clearly stated; is there a need for control group designs to compare outcomes; are probability statistics required to measure chance occurrences; and should there be a role for placebos in a double-blind study before conclusions are drawn? Learning to evaluate a scientific approach is an important critical thinking tool when hearing about research.

Here's a story about unroasted (green) coffee beans and weight reduction. In 2012, TV personality Dr. Mehmet Oz exclaimed: "Green Coffee Bean Extract: The Fat Burner That Works!" Based on the idea that these green coffee beans contain chlorogenic acid, which acts as an antioxidant to reduce blood sugar levels and possibly lead to weight loss, Dr. Oz touted a study that was eventually retracted from an open-access journal (Vinson, Burnham, and Nagendran, 2012). This study had the appearance of scientific methodology but on closer inspection turned out to be based on poorly designed pseudoscience methods.

Only 16 subjects from India between the ages of 22 and 46 who exhibited preobesity (as measured by BMI, the body mass index) participated in the study. They were divided randomly into three groups, each of which varied in the sequence of taking capsules for 22 weeks containing either green coffee bean extract with chlorogenic acid or a placebo. One group ($n = 6$) began with a high-dose/low-dose/placebo sequence; another group ($n = 4$) followed a low-dose/placebo/high-dose sequence; and the third group ($n = 6$) had a placebo/high-dose/low-dose sequence. Results indicated that all three groups had lost weight at the end of the trial period. The authors, however, said that the subjects lost more weight during the weeks when they were taking the green coffee extract, even though they still lost weight during the placebo period.

What critical thinking questions would you ask to get at the integrity of this research? The three comparison groups were so small in size, it's difficult to know if weight loss was due to the coffee extract or to simply engaging in daily diet monitoring. BMI is also not the best method for monitoring weight loss. Furthermore, despite the claim that it was a randomized double-blind study, there was no separate control group with placebo; each group was its own control group (Gavura, 2012). For these design flaws and other ethical reasons, the paper was eventually retracted.

And it's not just green coffee beans allegedly hosting these magical powers; at one time or another, blueberries, red wine, açaí berry, pomegranates, fish with omega-3 fatty acids, probiotic-filled yogurt, oat bran, kale, and green tea have also held the superfood crown. While many of these items do have benefits for a healthy life, understanding what makes some studies scientific and not just anecdotal requires applying critical thinking tools.

It is not unusual in today's social media world to hear about the curative powers of various foods, the incredible health benefits of certain vitamins, and the wonders of some new, secret, gluten-free diet plan. Questionable studies and sensational advertising touting all sorts of secret ingredients for weight, hair, or memory loss are widely available. Along with claims of paranormal occurrences, near-death experiences, UFO appearances, urban-legend truths, and conspiracy-theory beliefs, the media reports and personal stories many of us post and pass along can justifiably be called, at best, only entertainment and, at worst, pseudoscientific thinking.

We need to look more closely at the methodologies propping up these anecdotes, miraculous cures, and questionable surveys. Distinguishing quality scientific research from pseudoscience is essential, especially when the reports are focused on social and political issues impacting our daily lives, such as climate change, school curricula, gun control, and public health, to name a few. Let's begin by understanding what pseudoscience is before turning to the key components of scientific thinking and methodology.

PSEUDOSCIENCE

According to the National Science Board (2014: 7–25): "In 2012, about half of Americans (55%) said astrology is 'not at all scientific.'

One-third (32%) said they thought astrology was 'sort of scientific,' and 10% said it was 'very scientific.'" Four years earlier, 62 percent said it was not scientific, according to the General Social Survey (GSS) data. *What may these beliefs indicate about American's knowledge of science?*

Pseudoscientific thinking may have the appearance of science, but it includes, as Kida (2006) describes, these characteristics:

- Preconceived notions of what to believe.
- Searching for evidence to support a preconceived belief.
- Ignoring evidence that would falsify a claim or belief.
- Disregarding alternative explanations for a phenomenon.
- Holding extraordinary beliefs.
- Accepting flimsy evidence to support an extraordinary claim.
- Relying heavily on anecdotal evidence.
- Lacking tightly controlled experiments to test a claim.
- Employing very little skepticism.

Critical thinking means reviewing these characteristics when reading or hearing claims made in the news, on the Internet, and in published studies. For example, one listed item warns about a heavy reliance on *anecdotal evidence*. As discussed in chapter 2, anecdotes are information collected from small, often biased samples chosen to support some claim or product, especially a health-related one. Although anecdotal reports may lead to creating good research questions and hypotheses, such testimonials are not typically collected systematically with reliable and valid measurements. In many cases, especially in advertising, anecdotes usually imply causal connections among a limited set of variables without first establishing the necessary conditions to claim causality (as described in chapter 5).

Too often, we look for simple explanations to explain complex behaviors and opinions. So if after taking a dose of echinacea a cold comes to an end, attributing a cause-effect connection without considering alternative plausible explanations is a step in the direction of pseudoscientific thinking. In discussing anecdotes in a health-related investigation, Novella (2008) says:

CRITICAL THINKING TIP

Are testimonials the key aspects of the report or news item you are reading? Ask what is being measured, how it is assessed, who is participating in the study, how are the participants selected, and who is sponsoring the research. Is there a control group, and has the study been replicated? Be inquisitive if a complex behavioral outcome is explained by a simple, often one-item, treatment or cause.

An anecdote is a story—in the context of medicine it often relates to an individual's experience with their disease or symptoms and their efforts to treat it. . . . Whether or not a treatment works for a symptom or disease is a good example. Symptoms tend to vary over time, some may spontaneously remit, and our perceptions of symptoms are susceptible to a host of psychological factors. There are also numerous biological factors that may have an effect. If we are to make reliable decisions about the effects of specific interventions on symptoms and diseases we will need to do better than uncontrolled observation, or anecdotes.

Consider another characteristic in Kida's list: "Searching for evidence to support a preconceived belief." This characteristic of pseudoscience is referred to as *confirmation bias,* a tendency to focus more on ideas, events, and recollections that reinforce already-held beliefs. (See chapter 3.) It is related to such cognitive ideas as selective perception, selective recall, and selective exposure. Consider the everyday conversations you hear and the urban legends you receive in social media arguing for a causal connection between a full moon and an increase in emergency hospitalizations, births, suicides, binge drinking, werewolves, and criminal behavior. Yet researchers (Kelly, Rotton, and Culver, 1996) who reviewed more than 100 studies on lunar effects, concluded there was no reliable correlation between a full moon and such outcomes as epilepsy, domestic violence, homicides, or psychiatric admissions.

And of course, as we learned in chapter 5, even if there were a correlation, it certainly would not indicate causation. Perhaps confirmation bias may be a plausible alternative explanation. People in emergency rooms or police stations, for example, may be less likely to notice a full moon when there aren't many patients or crimes, less likely to recall at a later time the size of the moon when there are many emergencies, and less selectively attentive on other days when the moon is not full. *What other skeptical questions would you ask when hearing these urban legends?*

CRITICAL THINKING TIP

Ask yourself how often you selectively perceive, selectively remember, and selectively seek out information that confirms your already-held positions. When reading research or listening to others' views, evaluate not just their studies or opinions but your own ideas that filter what you are interpreting. How much confirmation bias is involved in your skeptical inquiry?

Pseudoscience is about the misuse of scientific methodology that can result in an absence of reliable and valid evidence. Some writers make a distinction between it and the *paranormal:* a set of beliefs beyond the scope of science. Goode (2012: 21, original italics) argues that "paranormalism is *a nonscientific or extrascientific approach to a phenomenon*—an event that contradicts what scientists take to be the laws of science." Understanding why some people and some cultures hold such beliefs is a different project than investigating the empirical evidence of paranormal claims. When your goal is to search for the validity of paranormal events—for example, ESP, séances, faith healings, reincarnation, psychic predictions, or the Bermuda Triangle—then the methods of scientific and critical thinking become more salient.

SCIENTIFIC METHODS

Many scientific research designs are available, and all depend on certain characteristics that distinguish them from nonscientific approaches. There is no one scientific method; it's about how science is practiced and adopted for different disciplines, research questions, and ethical standards. Scientific research can be designed for several purposes, including

- *explore* a new topic as a preliminary step for a more in-depth study,
- *describe* social behavior and opinions,
- *explain* social phenomena and cause-and-effect relationships,
- *predict* future behavior and opinions once they have been described and explained.

Each of these goals requires a methodology suited to achieving the particular purpose of the research. Critical thinking involves identifying the main goals of the project and evaluating the relationship between those research goals and the scientific elements needed to carry them out successfully. Several key principles characterize scientific methods, not all of which apply to all research designs. And in actual practice, science is an iterative process, sometimes of trial and error, unexpected findings, and serendipity, and often not following the linear pattern presented in standard definitions of science. The critical thinker needs to ask which of the following elements are relevant for determining whether what is reported in the media or published reports is scientific:

- Systematic design,
- Testable hypotheses,
- Reliable and valid measurements or observations,
- Replication,
- Control of alternative explanations,
- Random probability sampling for some research,
- For experiments: double-blind control groups, randomization, and placebos.

CRITICAL THINKING TIP

Seek out the methods used to collect the data quoted in published studies and media reports. First ask what the purpose of the study is, then evaluate the scientific elements that are required methodologically to achieve the goals of that project. Be suspicious of the absence of detailed descriptions of how the research was conducted. Even if you're not replicating the work, is there enough detail for you to carry out a similar research design?

Let's discuss these characteristics of a scientific method and how you can use them to critically evaluate reports of research and distinguish scientific studies from pseudoscientific claims. We begin with a study that illustrates not only the scientific process but also the way it evolved when two researchers read a book that struck them as needing some scientific verification. (What follows is based on Hart and Chabris,

2016.) Let the following example serve as a guide to how you can use critical thinking and apply the elements of a scientific methodology when reading research in scholarly publications or the popular media.

In 2014, law professors Amy Chua and Jed Rubenfeld published *The Triple Package: How Three Unlikely Traits Explain the Rise and Fall of Cultural Groups in America*. The authors focused their book on why certain groups (for example, Chinese, Jews, and Nigerians) achieve higher socioeconomic status in life than other groups. Their argument emphasized three traits: impulse control, personal insecurity, and a sense of group superiority. Individuals from cultural groups that socialize their children with these traits tend to be more successful in terms of higher education and income (socioeconomic status). The implication of their theoretical idea is that the interaction of the three traits leading to success is not limited to the specific groups Chua and Rubenfeld discuss; the theory should also be applicable to any individuals raised with these personality and social characteristics.

Needless to say, the media had a field day with this thesis, generating much publicity for the book as well as controversy about child-rearing practices, cultural influences, and "model minorities" issues. *At first glance, with just this very brief summary, what do your critical thinking tools alert you to about the book's ideas? What methods would you use to deduce some hypotheses and carry out a research project to evaluate them?*

One critic (Roithmayr, 2014) wrote that "the cultural arguments in the book aren't serious, more entertaining anecdote . . . than well-supported science. Of course *The Triple Package* isn't really serious scholarship, notwithstanding the authors' impressive credentials." Another writer (Deresiewicz, 2014) felt that "Chua and Rubenfeld do not explore alternative explanations, nor do they evaluate potential counterexamples" and that "evidence is comparably thin." Recall that one of the indicators of pseudoscientific reports is a dependence on anecdotal evidence.

Many critics of the book noticed this dependence on stories about cultural differences and child-rearing patterns rather than any kind of systematic data collection. They also called attention to the problematic ways that the three traits had not been clearly and consistently defined. Are rules of rabbinic law, resisting temptation, and self-subordination considered "impulse control"? What exactly is a sense of group superiority? Is it the same as ethnocentrism? And what are feelings of inferiority? Maybe low self-esteem or cultural persecution? How do you assess "success in life"? *Instead of using anecdotes, how would you measure these characteristics with some reliability and validity?*

Driven to do something about a fascinating research question concerning what makes some people more successful than others, the psychology professors Joshua Hart and Christopher Chabris (2016) decided to use Chua and Rubenfeld's theory to conduct a scientific study and critically evaluate the relationship among these three traits and success. The methods that Hart and Chabris use in their published research illustrate the scientific method and show clearly how critical thinking works in guiding them to go beyond anecdotes. In so doing, they demonstrate the crucial differences between pseudoscience and scientific methodology.

Systematic Design

A scientific project may begin with some casual observations, from ideas that pop into your head or from questions that come to mind when reading studies and media reports, as it did for Hart and Chabris with the Triple Package model espoused by Chua and Rubenfeld. Yet, what makes a research plan scientific is the development of some *systematic* methods to investigate those observations, informal ideas, and unanswered questions. Scientific research requires an organized plan or design demonstrating that it is not based on anecdotal and informal methodology. The components of the research plan should be specifically detailed enough for others to replicate the research.

In their published article, Hart and Chabris detailed their methodology for two studies they conducted testing the Triple Package ideas, including how they obtained their representative cross-sectional samples ($n = 430$ for Study One, and $n = 828$ for Study Two), measured the concepts, and statistically analyzed the data. For example, "Participants completed surveys of personality traits first, cognitive ability variables second, 'success' variables third, and demographic variables last" (Hart and Chabris, 2016: 217). This is not a haphazard, discursive study without a plan. For a qualitative or quantitative study to be scientific, it needs to be explicit about what it will be doing and how any changes in the research design are decided upon as the study moves along.

Testable Hypotheses

Fundamental to most scientific research is a set of research questions or hypotheses that predict some outcomes. A hypothesis is a proposed explanation of the relationships among variables based logically on prior research, observation, and sometimes intuition. For qualitative research, questions guide the study plan, even if not stated in hypothetical language. Hypotheses must be testable and refutable (sometimes called *falsifiable*): that is, they must be about phenomena that can be measured, tested experimentally, or observed, not something that is supernatural or paranormal. And they must allow the possibility of being shown to be false because, technically, science does not prove; it only fails to disprove. As Goode argues (2012: 77, original italics), paranormal statements "are very *rarely* falsifiable," and "scientific thinking . . . is *usually* falsifiable." On a practical level, however, "falsifiability of a theory is only one virtue; confirmability is even more important . . . science—and the theories that guide our daily lives— change mostly by generating supporting evidence, not by discovering falsifying evidence" (Nisbett, 2015: 264).

As an example, let's say you hypothesize that there are no yellow-dotted elephants in existence. Since it's impossible to survey every single elephant, a random sample is taken, and we observe there are no yellow-dotted elephants in that sample. So we accept our null hypothesis that there are none. Should we find such elephants in a sample, we reject our null hypothesis and say there exist such amazing creatures. Until we do (and good luck at that), we have not really proven our null hypothesis that they don't exist but have instead—using repeated samples— failed to disprove there aren't any. We succeed in disproving the null hypothesis when we find some. If there is a possibility that we may find a yellow-dotted elephant (or Bigfoot, the Loch Ness monster, etc.)— thereby disproving the hypothesis that such creatures don't exist—then we can say our research hypothesis or question has the characteristic of being falsifiable.

Returning to the Triple Package idea, Hart and Chabris (2016: 217) state Chua and Rubenfeld's book's hypothesis as "group superiority combined with insecurity leads to 'drive,' which is ineffectual without 'grit,' or the determination to persevere in the face of obstacles; grit is purportedly derived from a combination of superiority and impulse control. In turn, the combination of drive and grit create success." They fault the book for basing its argument on "evidence that consists mostly of anecdotes . . . or simple descriptive statistics," and state that the original book has "imprecise definitions of constructs," which fail to specify whether the three traits are additive or multiplicatively interactive.

In other words, the original book presents a hypothesis but does not specify how to operationalize the concepts or collect evidence systematically. Therefore it does not have some key characteristics of a scientific study; rather the book's premise provides the opportunity for conducting a proper scientific study.

Reliable and Valid Measurements

What makes scientific research systematic involves providing details about how concepts are measured or observed in a study. It's not clear in the Triple Package study what exactly is meant, for example, by a belief in a group's superiority, let alone how it may be observed or assessed. *How would you measure it if you were designing this research?* Hart and Chabris decided to use a published 22-item Revised Ethnocentrism Scale to measure the concept in their attempt to be more scientific. Note that using this scale was a choice made by the researchers and was not spelled out by the original Triple Package theory. Someone else could do a similar test of the theory by deciding to measure a sense of group exceptionalism in another way. Selecting a method of measurement is called *operationalizing* the variables.

Hart and Chabris similarly spelled out their measures for insecurity and impulse control, using various scales and multiple indicators of these traits. Given that their goal was to explain success (which can be defined in numerous ways), Hart and Chabris (2016: 218) chose Chua and Rubenfeld's definition, which emphasizes income, status, and prestige, and created a composite measure as well as ones for each of those elements: "We asked participants to report their annual income (in increments of $20,000, up to $80,000, and then in increments of $40,000 to 'greater than $200,000'), and their highest level of education (seven options, from 'Grade school or less' to 'Graduate/professional degree)." *In what other ways could you measure these concepts and variables?*

More important, Hart and Chabris (2016: 218) provide data on the reliability of the scales used in their study. For example, the Revised Ethnocentrism Scale has a very high (0.93) reliability coefficient, indicating that it is consistently measuring ethnocentrism. When reviewing research, be alert to indicators that the tools used to operationalize the concepts and variables of the study are reliable and valid. (See also chapter 5.)

CRITICAL THINKING TIP

Ask if what you are reviewing illustrates a systematic methodology. Are hypotheses or research questions guiding the
study? Is there a discussion of how subjects were selected for
the project? Are measurement methods detailed sufficiently
to understand how concepts have been operationalized with
some reliability and validity?

Replication

Even with reliable and valid findings, research remains *tentative:* that is,
it is open to further investigation. Recall that research does not prove
hypotheses directly but fails to disprove them. Data analysis is also
based on probability, rather than 100 percent certainty, as discussed in
chapter 3. Additional evidence is often required to secure the original
findings, build on them, modify them, or even correct them when information is uncovered that falsifies them.

Tentativeness also provides a way of distinguishing science from pseudoscience. According to Timmer (2006):

> Many forms of pseudoscience, such as creationism, strive to squeeze data
> into support of a pre-ordained and invariant conclusion. Others, such as
> belief in UFO abductions, persist despite extensive counterevidence. In light
> of this, one potential way to gain a sense of how scientific a concept is would
> be to ask one of its proponents what pieces of data would cause them to
> modify or discard their favored model.

Finding data to modify or discard a theory occurs through seeking replication. See it as a type of reliability: consistency of results across multiple
research studies. Replication requires following the methods described in
a research project and either altering small elements (for example, does a
study get similar or different results with a sample of non–college students
in comparison with an original study's college students?) or reproducing a
study a second time with the exact same measurements and sampling.

Consider a project that attempted to replicate 100 psychology studies
that were published in three academic journals. The Open Science Collaboration (2015: 943) group found that "A large portion of replications
produced weaker evidence for the original findings." Only 36 percent of
the replications had significant results. Yet, in a rebuttal to this investigation, Gilbert et al. (2016) analyzed the replication data of the Open Science Collaboration project and stated that "the data are consistent with

the opposite conclusion, namely, that the reproducibility of psychological science is quite high." These researchers believe that replication was successful in almost 60 percent of the studies. In either case, replication is a necessary component of the scientific process and remains a controversial issue in the social sciences.

Many times, researchers attempt to replicate their study before announcing or publishing their results in order to guarantee some reliability in their findings. A critical thinker asks this question about replication: *When you read about the latest food that is supposed to be good or bad for you, is there any indication that the findings have been replicated, or is this the one-and-only study that says coffee, or blueberries, or kale will add years to your longevity?*

Hart and Chabris replicated their research before publication. They repeated their own study with a sample size twice that of the original: "Study 2 followed the same procedure as Study 1, but with some measures omitted to minimize the demands on participants while still conceptually replicating Study 1" (2016: 220). Study 2's results duplicated the findings of Study 1 and found that the Triple Package hypotheses of Chua and Rubenfeld could not be supported (Hart and Chabris, 2016: 221):

> Across two studies with sizable samples of U.S. adults (N = 1,258), we found that achievement of awards, education, and income was predicted by the educational attainment of individuals' parents (a proxy for socioeconomic status) and individuals' own cognitive ability as estimated by brief verbal and math tests. However, we found scant support for a 'Triple Package' hypothesis that a group superiority complex (i.e., ethnocentrism), personal insecurity (operationalized in four different ways), and impulse control interact to predict exceptional achievement."

CRITICAL THINKING TIP

Is there any evidence of the study's being replicated by other researchers? If so, in what ways was the project duplicating the original study, how was it modified, and did the results replicate or alter the initial findings? Is there confidence in the research findings if it has yet to be replicated?

Control of Alternative Explanations

As discussed in chapter 5, correlations require several conditions before causation can be declared, including ruling out alternative explanations.

Critically evaluating media reports and scientific studies involves raising questions about other possible reasons for the findings. The use of control groups in classic experimental research designs is the primary scientific method for investigating alternative explanations for this type of study. Qualitative research, on the other hand, can include observations and interviews about other plausible factors in order to address alternative explanations. However, for some studies (such as cross-sectional surveys) evaluating the role of other explanations can be accomplished through data analysis techniques by statistically controlling for specific variables.

This is what Hart and Chabris did by collecting data on parents' educational attainment to control for socioeconomic status (SES) when their subjects were growing up. They also introduced a cognitive ability measurement (a composite of mathematical and reading test scores), since that is typically related to success. And, as they discovered, parental SES and cognitive ability were statistically stronger predictors of success than the three variables posited in the Chua and Rosenfeld book.

By including alternative explanations, researchers can discover stronger relationships, nullify other findings, and begin to explain causality. Pseudoscience, however, rarely controls for additional variables that may be related to the outcomes under scrutiny. *What would be some alternative explanations of UFO abductions or Bigfoot sightings?*

Experiments: Randomization, Double-Blind, and Placebo Control Groups

As discussed in chapter 2, the ideal scientific research design, especially for quantitative studies focused on explanations and causality, requires random probability sampling. When distributing surveys or collecting data, it's best to avoid convenience samples and to find representative participants that allow for making more accurate scientific inferential generalizations about the population. Since qualitative methods and other observational case studies do not regularly depend on random samples, their strength is in providing in-depth exploratory and descriptive findings limited to the sample studied.

However, when designing experiments, randomization is an essential component of the scientific methodology. The gold standard experimental design, especially for epidemiological and medical research, involves randomized double-blind placebo control (RDBPC) methods. Pseudoscientific claims and studies like the one for Dr. Oz's green coffee beans tend to avoid these gold standard research designs.

CRITICAL THINKING TIP

Especially when reading about the numerous reports implying wonderful outcomes from vitamins, foods, magical cures, look for the gold standard model of randomized control groups, use of placebos, and double-blind methods. Ask how well the research design described in the report or study can rule out plausible alternative explanations.

Experiments involve conditions in which the researcher can manipulate the conditions to test out the effects of independent variables on some dependent or outcome variables. Seeking to explain relationships and establish causation, experiments require:

- a treatment/experimental group (that receives the independent variables),
- a control group (that either does not get the treatment or else receives a placebo version),
- random assignment of subjects to the control and treatment groups,
- measures both before and after the treatment or placebo,
- no knowledge by either the subjects or the researchers as to which participants are in the treatment or the control group (known as double-blind procedure).

We've mentioned placebos several times already. A *placebo* (Latin for "I will please") is a substance or procedure given to a *control group* to compare with an equivalent *treatment group* receiving the real intervention or pill. In medical research, the look-alike placebo is often a sugar pill that does not have any real effect on the condition being studied, allowing comparisons to be made between the actual medicine and the fake one. For other kinds of research, a control group can simply be the absence of some treatment or, when using a placebo, some benign equivalent treatment.

It's fairly common for about a third of people in a placebo control group to report positive changes or lessening of symptoms (Carroll, 2003). Some patients even when told outright that they had received a fake, placebo, treatment continue to report positive outcomes. Occasionally, recipients of a placebo claim negative side-effects (the *nocebo* effect), such as headaches or nausea. In a study from New Zealand, for example, university students who were told they were drinking vodka and tonic, but were really sipping a tonic-only placebo, acted drunk, demonstrated worse eyewitness accounts, and were more easily swayed by misleading information (Assefi and Garry, 2003). Similarly, many people in a placebo group reported gastrointestinal problems when participating in a study of gluten sensitivity even after consuming gluten-free food (Biesiekierski, Muir, and Gibson, 2013).

When reviewing research and media reports, it's important to critically think out what role placebos play or should play in a study. Oster (2015) states the impact that placebos can have on gluten sensitivities research as an example:

> It's difficult to distinguish between someone who is sensitive to gluten and someone who is sensitive to the placebo effect. Since there is no test for gluten sensitivity, "diagnoses" are based on whether people say they feel better when they avoid gluten. But the mind is a powerful thing. If you think avoiding gluten will make you feel better, there is a reasonable chance that it will—even if gluten is irrelevant.

Now consider this research design about the efficacy of acupuncture in relieving pain after a wisdom tooth extraction: "One hundred and twenty patients were randomly assigned to one of three groups: an experimental group consisting of those receiving real acupuncture and two placebo groups" (Bausell, 2007: 116). One placebo group (n = 40) received four fake acupuncture needle insertion sensations and one very shallow insertion, whereas the other placebo group (n = 40) received four very shallow insertions and one insertion sensation. The experimental group (n = 40) received true acupuncture needle insertions in the same locations as the placebo groups but with the greater depth required by traditional Chinese practice. All subjects' eyes were covered to avoid seeing the real or fake needle insertions. *With just this limited information, how would you evaluate the research methods so far?*

Results showed no significant differences in the average scores on a pain scale experienced between the acupuncture treatment group and the two placebo control groups. To replicate the research, a modified follow-up study using one placebo group (n = 120) instead of two and a larger acupuncture group (n = 60) confirmed similar findings: "There was no difference between real and fake acupuncture with respect to the average amount of pain experienced" (Bausell, 2007: 118). In addition, the researchers discovered that patients who thought they were receiving real acupuncture—regardless of whether they were in the actual or fake acupuncture groups—reported experiencing significantly less dental pain. *What does this suggest about placebos?*

Although this brief summary of the study does not provide more in-depth findings and other research design elements, the point is to demonstrate what to look for when critically thinking about research and the basic components of a scientific methodology. *What makes this study a scientific one, rather than the anecdotal writings or pseudoscience studies found in many public media about the efficacy of acupuncture to relieve pain?*

OTHER SCIENTIFIC METHODS

Not all quality scientific research fits the randomized double-blind placebo control (RDBPC) design model of interventional experiments. Although that may be what many label the gold standard when testing new products, medicines, diets, and related health issues, it is often not possible to assign people randomly into groups or even to provide placebo treatments. Yet these research designs could still represent scientific thinking.

Especially for epidemiological topics, research methods can involve such designs as observing population trends in reported cases of an illness, such as incidence (the probability of occurrence in a population of heart attacks, for example) and prevalence (the proportion of people considered obese in a population). Another study could evaluate emergency room admission records and analyze the time of day, day of the week, and the type of medical issue to reach some conclusions about patterns or anomalies. These descriptive studies can be cross-sectional, at one point in time, or longitudinal, comparing trends over months or years.

Other epidemiological studies ask participants to recall past behaviors or opinions. These *retrospective case-controlled* designs may begin with some health condition today—for example, lung cancer—and then ask lung cancer patients about behaviors that occurred leading up to the current condition, like nutritional patterns, exercise habits, and smoking rates. They can be compared to a control group of people without lung cancer to see how they differ on those variables. However, people are not randomly assigned to the case and control groups, since it would of course be unethical and impractical to ask a set of participants to enter a treatment group and start smoking and compare it with others randomly assigned to a no-smoking or placebo-cigarette control group!

Some research may begin with a current baseline survey and follow subjects who periodically complete follow-up questionnaires over time. This longitudinal design is a *cohort prospective* methodology and is best represented by the Nurses' Health Study (NHS). Originally developed in 1976 to investigate the long-term heart disease and cancer outcomes of contraceptive use and smoking, the NHS recruited female nurses to complete detailed surveys every two years. Almost 90 percent of the nurses continued to answer questions about diet, nutrition, and lifestyle issues in the follow-up surveys, making this prospective research one of the most successful and important longitudinal projects on women's health. (See Nurses Health Study, 2016, for a complete description of the methodology.)

Yet, it's important to keep in mind what Heather Gilligan (2015) wrote about nutritional science methodologies and the conflicting advice on which foods are good for us and which ones to avoid:

> Many nutritional studies are observational studies, including massive ones like the Nurses' Health Study. Researchers like [Harvard nutritionist Walter] Willett try to suss out how changes in diet affect health by looking at associations between what people report they eat and how long they live. When many observational studies reach the same conclusions, Willett says, there is enough evidence to support dietary recommendations. Even though they only show correlation, not cause and effect, observational studies direct what we eat. Apart from their inability to determine cause and effect, there's another problem with observational studies: The data they're based on—surveys where people report what they ate the day (or week) before—are notoriously unreliable. Researchers have long known that people (even nurses) misreport, intentionally and unintentionally, what they eat. Scientists politely call this "recall bias."

CRITICAL THINKING TIP

When reviewing the methodology designed for a study, ask if this is the design best suited for the research questions and hypotheses. Does it meet the criteria for classifying the research methods as scientific? How else could researchers study the issue, and with what other methods, to make it more acceptably scientific?

Growing exponentially in today's Internet-mediated world is the collection of so-called Big Data. *Big Data* refers to the massive amounts of data generated often through social media websites like Facebook and Twitter,

Google searches, Amazon shopping, Netflix selections, and other Internet-driven websites. Notice how when you use some sites, ads appear related to recent searches you made and predictions are provided of other books, shopping gifts, or movies you may enjoy. These items are the result of mathematical algorithms and instant data analyses based on collected and aggregated information gathered from users, all made possible by large computers capable of handling billions of data points simultaneously.

Issues emerge not only of privacy, but also ones related to the critical thinking methods discussed in this book about sampling, probability, and research design. It is possible to divide large databases into smaller subsamples to compare outcomes in what marketing people call classic *A/B testing*, as Netflix did by comparing 100,000 subscribers who received one version of the opening user interface screen (group A) compared with another 100,000 (group B) who saw a different version of the opening screen (Nocera, 2016). *What are the limitations and strengths of Big Data collection? Are these methods considered scientific?*

It's important when reading reports or hearing results from Big Data to critically ask: How well can nonrandom sampling lead to predictions of behavior and attitudes in larger populations when generalizability is most accurate with random probability sampling? How reliable and valid are the measurements used to collect the information? Can Big Data give us more than descriptive and exploratory findings when explanations and establishing causation are limited by the methodologies? Do such large data sets artificially make small differences statistically significant, leading to unwarranted conclusions and policies? Since these data sets are almost always based on populations, not samples, how generalizable are they to other populations? (See Mayer-Schonberger and Cukier, 2013, for a discussion of the pros and cons of Big Data.)

Another research method that's become increasingly popular is *meta-analysis*. Using systematic analyses, researchers pool data from numerous studies on the same topic to seek more powerful statistical findings, rather than base conclusions on fewer results. This technique can help avoid conflicting conclusions by uncovering patterns and providing stronger statistical power, especially important for studies dealing with health, epidemiology, and nutrition. For example, the Australian National Health and Medical Research Council (2015: 5) reviewed 1,800 research studies on homeopathy—the controversial complementary and alternative medical system—which believes diluted "substances that may cause illness or symptoms in a healthy person can, in very small doses, treat those symptoms in a person who is unwell." Focusing on 225 published articles meeting scientific standards, the meta-analysis concluded (2015: 6):

> There was no reliable evidence from research in humans that homeopathy was effective for treating the range of health conditions considered: no good-quality, well-designed studies with enough participants for a meaningful result reported either that homeopathy caused greater health improvements than placebo, or caused health improvements equal to those of another treatment. For some health conditions, studies reported that homeopathy was not more effective than placebo. . . . Homeopathy should not be used to treat health conditions that are chronic, serious, or could become serious. People who choose homeopathy may put their health at risk if they reject or delay treatments for which there is good evidence for safety and effectiveness.

As with other kinds of sampling, researchers using meta-analysis must make some decisions about which studies to include or exclude, what criteria are applied in selecting research, and how many years and data sets to use. It can be a scientific technique if the studies chosen for analysis meet scientific criteria. *Applying the critical thinking questions discussed, what other methodological issues does meta-analysis raise?*

While many of the types of studies described here do not employ the experimental scientific standard of randomized double-blind placebo control (RDBPC) designs, they remain important scientific methods for formulating hypotheses to be used in other studies, providing longitudinal descriptive data that may suggest relevant and possible causes of diseases in epidemiological research and answering some questions not possible with the more traditional experimental research design and smaller data sets.

Science is not some fixed method with a one-size-fits-all approach. What's important for the critical thinker is to ask the questions about the data collection methodologies, the scientific elements of the research, and whether the conclusions drawn are limited and relevant to the research questions asked. To understand what makes reports and claims scientific is to understand the differences from pseudoscience, anecdotes, and opinions, and not simply see the research as following a rigid checklist of objective techniques.

KEY TERMS

A/B TESTING Comparing two variations of something, often used in marketing to test reactions to different versions of a product.

ANECDOTAL STUDIES Studies collecting data from small, often biased, samples chosen to support some claim or issue.

BIG DATA Very large sets of data collected and analyzed with powerful computers to find patterns and trends.

CASE-CONTROLLED STUDIES Studies that begin by asking a group of subjects with a particular outcome to recall behaviors and exposure that may have led up to that outcome.

COHORT LONGITUDINAL DESIGN A method of study that begins with a baseline survey and follows subjects prospectively who periodically complete follow-up questionnaires over time.

CONFIRMATION BIAS A study flaw of selectively perceiving, recalling, and interpreting information that verifies already-held beliefs and views.

CONTROL GROUP A group of subjects not receiving a treatment and matched to a group receiving an experimental treatment.

GOLD STANDARD RESEARCH DESIGN Randomized double-blind placebo control method, or RDBPC.

HYPOTHESIS A proposed explanation of the relationships among variables based logically on prior research, observation, and sometimes intuition.

META-ANALYSIS Systematically combining data from selected studies to develop an overall finding that has greater statistical power than any one of them.

NOCEBO A noneffective substance whose use results in negative or harmful outcomes when employed in an experimental treatment.

PLACEBO A noneffective substance whose use results in a positive outcome or no outcome at all when employed in an experimental treatment.

PSEUDOSCIENCE A system of statements not following scientific procedures and often based on anecdotes.

REPLICATION Repetition of a research design to provide stronger confirmation of a finding.

SYSTEMATIC STUDY An organized research plan or design not based on anecdotal and informal methodology but with specifically detailed steps and procedures.

EXERCISES

1. Consider this case reported in the *New York Post* (Doyle, 2011): "A psychic eerily predicted where the victim of a suspected serial killer could be found—nine months before cops dug up the corpse . . . on a Long Island beach, police sources said." Claiming to see the body in a grave "overlooking a body of water" with a nearby sign that had the letter "G" in it, did the psychic really "nail it," as the newspaper said?

   (a) As critical thinkers, what questions do you ask about the success of this so-called psychic detective? (See Radford, 2011, for one person's response to this psychic's discovery).

   (b) Imagine you were hired to design a study testing the anecdotal evidence provided by media reports of psychic detectives. What would you do to make it a more scientific research design? (See Wiseman and West, 1996, for an example of a psychologist's study of psychic abilities.)

2. Selective attention and selective recall often impact how we interpret news, remember events, and experience everyday interactions. Here's a fun study asking how expectations affect real-time experiences, not just after-the-fact characterizations of an event. Bar patrons were approached in two local student bars and asked to participate in a short study involving free beer. Almost all ($n = 388$) agreed (Lee, Frederick, and Ariely, 2006: 1055):

> Respondents consumed two beer samples: one unadulterated sample and one sample of "MIT brew," which contained several drops of balsamic vinegar—a beer flavoring that most participants find conceptually offensive, but that does not, at this concentration, degrade the beer's flavor (in fact, it slightly improves it). Respondents were randomly assigned to one of three conditions. In the blind condition, they tasted the two samples without any information about the contents. In the before condition, they were told which beer contained balsamic vinegar, prior to tasting either. In the after condition, they first tasted the beers and were then told which beer contained balsamic vinegar.

   (a) Using the characteristics of scientific research, how would you evaluate this description of the research methodology?
   (b) What would you change in or add to the research design?
   (c) What kinds of additional research may be interesting to conduct based on the findings from this study that expectations often override experience?

> "The results across three experiments suggest that information (about the presence of a conceptually offensive ingredient) influences preferences more when received before consumption than when received after consumption.
>
> "The MIT brew was liked much less when disclosure preceded sampling than when respondents learned about the balsamic vinegar after they had tasted both samples" (Lee, Frederick, and Ariely, 2006: 1057).

CHAPTER 7

Fact, Opinion, and Logical Reasoning

Critical Thinking, Step Seven: What is the difference between a fact and an opinion? How do you decide what is fake news or reliable information derived from a scientific study? The media often claim to exhibit fairness and balance in their reports, but learning to evaluate these concepts requires some critical thinking tools and logical reasoning skills. Applying these tools and skills when confronting unusual media claims is an important last step in developing critical thinking expertise.

In the Disney animated movie *Inside Out,* the character Joy trips over two boxes, one labeled "facts" and another marked "opinion." The pieces in each box mix together. When Joy tries to remedy the situation and put them back into their proper containers, she exclaims, "These facts and opinions look so similar!" And comedian John Oliver said this about climate change debates: "You don't need people's opinion on a fact. You might as well have a poll asking: 'Which number is bigger, 15 or 5?' or 'Do owls exist?' or 'Are there hats?'"

Too often, we ourselves confuse fact with opinion and come to conclusions that are not logically connected to the factual findings. Let's explore these topics and use our critical thinking tools to evaluate interpretations, opinions, and facts as presented in research studies, polls, surveys, and everyday observations from the media.

Facts related to an issue are different from *opinions* about it. Making logical inferences from facts through *inductive* and *deductive reasoning* is not the same as expressing personal viewpoints. Being *uninformed* about a topic is different from being *misinformed* about it. Learning to distinguish such ideas is an indicator of successful critical thinking and a method for bringing together many of the key themes of the book.

FACT

Evidence is the key to distinguishing fact from opinion. A *fact* is something that has been derived from qualitative observation or quantitative evidence, that can be demonstrated to be true, and that can be done so without any bias involved. The dictionary defines it as a piece of information having an actual existence, an actual occurrence, and an objective reality. Despite this definition, it's not unusual to hear the word "fact" misused in everyday situations. *What do you think about when you hear the word "fact"?*

Way back when, *Dragnet* was a popular TV police show and movie whose Detective Sergeant Joe Friday used to say, "All we want are the facts, ma'am." Yet, eyewitness accounts, alibis from suspects, and police reports don't always report the same details with "objective reality." Consider this high school student whose senior prom was disrupted by a tornado and who concluded (as reported on *This American Life,* 2001) that "It's a known fact that our class since the fourth grade has been jinxed." Where's the unbiased evidence to support this "known fact," let alone any objective way to determine how "being jinxed" can be operationalized?

Lepore (2016) wrote that in today's society, disputes about facts are really arguments about what counts as evidence. Facts have been replaced by data (especially Big Data collected by technology); science is seen as a belief, with objectivity deemed an illusion. This wasn't always the case, as Lepore (2016) notes:

> In England, the abolition of trial by ordeal [in 1215] led to the adoption of trial by jury for criminal cases. This required a new doctrine of evidence and a new method of inquiry, and led to what the historian Barbara Shapiro has called "the culture of fact": the idea that an observed or witnessed act or thing—the substance, the matter, of fact—is the basis of truth and the only kind of evidence that's admissible not only in court but also in other realms where truth is arbitrated. Between the thirteenth century and the nineteenth, the fact spread from law outward to science, history, and journalism.

Journalists are especially cautioned about the use of facts in both written and visual forms. A photographer (van Agtmael, 2016) writing an opinion piece in *Time* magazine reminds us that even something as supposedly objective as a photo can be easily manipulated: "Style, lens choice, position, what to show and what to exclude in the framing, editing, equipment choice, toning, sequence are all manipulative and subjective. The result is a collection of facts that tends to be sanctimoniously declared as representing 'truth.'"

The News Manual (2012) guide for the media says reporters must learn how to distinguish fact from opinion "in both gathering and writing news. It affects how you deal with anything you are told and also how you pass the information on to your readers or listeners." *The News Manual* looks at three kinds of facts for people working in print and electronic media news: proven facts, probable facts, and probable lies.

Proven facts do not need supportive documentation since they are accepted as true and proven by everyone, like "Beyoncé is a singer." Whether you think she is a talented, mediocre, or bad singer is an opinion. *Probable facts* are ones that sound reasonably true but for which you yourself cannot provide the evidence. The media must attribute such a fact to a reliable source who is in a position to know the truth, like "the Census Bureau chief reported a 12 percent increase in Hispanics moving into the state last year." *Probable lies* may or may not be factual. *The News Manual* states, "People occasionally make statements which seem on the surface to be untrue, but which might just be true. . . . You must always check such statements before using them, and never use them without confirming them first" (*News Manual*, 2012).

CRITICAL THINKING TIP

When reading research, viewing online blogs, or hearing media reports, be attentive to the differences between proven facts, probable facts, and opinions. Learn to spot phrases, words, and styles that indicate a personal bias or interpretation that is not derived from the evidence and objective data.

Journalists and other media people are not the only ones needing to understand the meaning of facts. Researchers are also required when reporting findings to clearly make statements that derive from the data in an unbiased way. Presenting a finding that says, "20 percent of college students did not vote in the last election," is a fact when supported by evidence from a scientific exit poll, but it becomes opinion if stated as "a *disappointing* 20 percent of the students did not vote in the last election." Factual information in a presentation or academic research summary can easily slip into personal opinion with careless use of adjectives and labels suggesting a particular viewpoint. This opinionated reporting can also be a result of confirmation bias and selective perception. (See chapter 3.) *When was the last time you qualified a fact with an opinionated adjective?*

As discussed in chapter 6, scientific results are typically stated in a probabilistic way, since science cannot always determine with 100 percent certainty that the facts are fixedly established. Occasionally information is in a state between facts and opinions, or studies report contradictory findings, all awaiting replication and verification.

OPINION

It's impossible to see the world around us without feelings and emotions. Our views on issues and sentiments about people and events are our *opinions.* They may or may not be based on facts, because opinions are personal, subjective judgments and emotions. The name of the highest-grossing movie of the week is a fact supported by box-office evidence; your feelings about that film are your opinion. *Can you think of an example you recently heard or read (especially in Comments sections of social media) that mixed fact with opinion?*

True news segments, whether written, televised, or interactive, will rely on facts and sourcing in order to provide information to the reader or viewer. An opinion piece, particularly about a newsworthy issue, will be informed by facts but will allow one particular stance or viewpoint to shine through in order to persuade the reader to agree with the opinion. Identifying opinions is easily done by looking for interpretive labels ("good," "bad," etc.) and words like "probably," "sometimes," "I think," or "I believe."

When there appears to be consensus about an issue or topic, opinions about it can look like fact. Consider the number of times you have been part of a group that holds a very strong opinion about a subject, like vaccines cause autism despite scientific evidence to the contrary. (See Jain, Marshall, and Buikema, 2015.) Within the group, this opinion may eventually seem factual. Yet, what may sound like an opinion is often misinformation about a topic. *If you believe that climate change is a hoax, is that an opinion, or is it factual misinformation?*

As Nisbett wrote (2015: 32):

Remember that all perceptions, judgments, and beliefs are inferences and not direct readouts of reality. This recognition should prompt an appropriate humility about just how certain we should be about our judgments, as well as a recognition that the views of other people that differ from our own may have more validity than our intuitions tell us they do.

MISINFORMATION

Just because a study or research design is scientifically valid and reliable does not guarantee that the interpretations derived from the findings are free from opinion or bias. In the ideal world, facts should provide a foundation for our beliefs. Yet we know that opinions can determine which facts we selectively perceive, attend to, and recall. Confirmation bias illustrates how we seek out information supporting already-held beliefs. But what if those beliefs are incorrect?

We're not talking about the *uninformed*—people who have little or no information, data, or research about an issue or topic. For example, not being able to name the major denominations of Islam and distinguish Shiites from Sunnis is being uninformed about that religion. Education and experience are tools to improve learning for the uninformed. The *misinformed,* on the other hand, are people who speculate or believe demonstrably false data, like the 41 percent of adults who think, for example, that the earliest humans and dinosaurs lived at the same time, as a national survey commissioned by the California Academy of Sciences (2009) discovered. Or the CNN poll (Agiesta, 2015) that found that 29 percent of adults surveyed believe ex-President Barack Obama is a Muslim.

Misinformation has consequences in creating a culture of fear, as Glassner (1999: 208) explained: "Statements of alarm by newscasters and glorification of wannabe experts are two telltale tricks of the fear mongers' trade . . . [and of] others as well: the use of poignant anecdotes in place of scientific evidence, the christening of isolated incidents as trends, depictions of entire categories of people as innately dangerous."

Fake news has become an increasingly problematic feature in today's social media and Internet sites. (See Agrawal, 2016.) Whereas most people know to take so-called news appearing on *The Daily Show* or in *The Onion* as humor or satire, when stories are purposely written to misinform without comedic intent, it becomes difficult to distinguish the real from the fake. This kind of misinformation has been around in

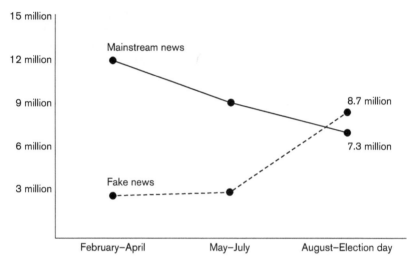

FIGURE 29. Total Facebook engagements for top 20 presidential election stories, 2016. (BuzzFeed News.)

various forms before, especially as propaganda during wartime or other political conflicts, but its proliferation during the 2016 U.S. presidential election caused concern serious enough for Facebook and Google to begin implementing plans to control it. As figure 29 indicates, Facebook users shared, commented on, or reacted to election news stories from fake news sites more often than from mainstream media ones.

Despite attempts to counteract fake news on such fact-checking websites as Snopes.com or Politifact.com, consider how misinformation may persist even when interpreting facts that contradict already-held opinions. Nyhan and Reifler (2010) found that undergraduate college students who were misinformed about political issues persisted in their beliefs and sometimes held on to them even more strongly (the so-called backfire effect) despite being presented with corrected facts. They concluded (2010: 323, original italics): "We find that responses to corrections in mock news articles differ significantly according to subjects' ideological views. As a result, the corrections fail to reduce misperceptions for the most committed participants. Even worse, they actually *strengthen* misperceptions among ideological subgroups in several cases."

Using our beliefs to determine which facts to seek out and interpret can lead us to be less critical with incomplete and erroneous information. It could also result in ignoring new information and increasing our confidence that our opinions are correct. Keohane (2010) wrote: "This effect is only heightened by the information glut, which offers—alongside an unprecedented amount of good information—endless rumors, misinformation, and questionable variations on the truth. In other words, it's never been easier for people to be wrong, and at the same time feel more certain that they're right."

CRITICAL THINKING TIP

When reading or hearing research or news reports, ask yourself whether you are receptive to alternative interpretations available in sources that differ from your ideological perspective. Do you overlook the missing or problematic elements of good scientific methodology—that is, become a less critical thinker—when reinforcing your already-held opinions?

Besides ignoring conflicting information, people tend to reinforce their opinions and misinformation by retreating to positions that cannot be investigated scientifically: that is, unfalsifiable, untestable positions. Recall (in chapter 6) how hypotheses should be able to be shown to be refutable and false. Otherwise, we may find ourselves in the realm of paranormal or pseudoscientific studies.

Friesen, Campbell, and Kay (2015: 517) researched how "framing one's beliefs in more unfalsifiable terms may make those beliefs less subject to disconfirmation." They found that people will claim scientific facts are just nonrefutable opinion when they contradict their beliefs. It often has been the case that people critique the methodology of studies that challenge their opinions, but now invocations of moral opinion are increasingly used, especially for political and religious issues (such as capital punishment, abortion, same-sex marriage). Such framing prevents evidence-based research and the development of falsifiable studies to determine facts. Friesen, Campbell, and Kay conclude (2015: 523):

> When one holds a political position and encounters facts that appear to contradict that position, the rational response would be to revise one's belief to be more in line with the new information. Instead, when faced with threatening information, both proponents and opponents of same-sex marriage reported that the political issues of same-sex marriage and parenting were less about "facts" and more matters of moral opinion. In other words, they protected their political beliefs by framing the issue as more unfalsifiable.

FAIRNESS AND BALANCE

As anyone who has ever watched television news knows, endless debates about controversial topics characterize cable shows. Partly because of journalistic ethics prescribing that reporters must demonstrate fairness by providing balance, viewers get to experience shouting matches and occasional serious debates among competing perspectives. Usually these arguments develop from a "two-sides-of-the-coin" belief (when in reality there are probably multiple views). *Are a range of positions given fair and balanced treatment when you read or watch the news?*

Despite engaging with alternative ideas, as mentioned earlier, we tend to listen selectively and employ confirmation bias in reinforcing our already-held opinions. What should be interpretations deduced from data and presentations of facts typically turn out to be shouting contests of opinions. A critical thinker needs to discern these opinions, attend to the different facts, and decide what a fair and balanced approach to an issue is. Not all topics require this, of course; you wouldn't have a member of the Ku Klux Klan balance someone highlighting hate crimes against ethnic and racial minorities.

When engaging with news stories, research, and media reports, it's important to critically evaluate in what ways fairness and balance may be misused. For example,

- Just because two sides of a story are presented does not necessarily mean the truth is in the middle.
- Objectivity in gathering information is almost always affected by some subjective elements of those people collecting, interpreting, and disseminating the facts. Often just the choice of what to report or research is reflective of someone's preferences and biases.
- When established views or facts are questioned by some group or individual protesting the status quo, media often then seek out commentary from established leaders and officials, thereby reinforcing conventional wisdom and power positions.
- Reporting of controversial events with balance may seem fair unless the language, visuals, and commentary used in introducing various positions are loaded with consciously chosen or inadvertent bias (like speaking of "the so-called leader" or averring that a murder was committed by a "thug" or a "terrorist" or a "loner").

- Balance should not be limited to only two positions of a contested issue. Multiple perspectives are often ignored when a topic is reduced to simple pro and con arguments.

One of the problems with balance in the media is that it can distort the proportion of opposing views. When two sides are given equal treatment, viewers may assume a 50–50 split on important topics, thereby creating a false impression. Koehler (2016: 11) found in his research that "false balance (i.e., presenting both sides of an issue when in fact one side is overwhelmingly supported by the majority of experts) can distort public opinion by inflating perceptions of disagreement and uncertainty among experts." For example, despite 97 percent agreement among scientists (in published peer-reviewed articles taking a position) that human activity causes global warming and climate change, less than half of the respondents in a Pew Research study thought scientists agreed on this subject. Nuccitelli (2013) says:

> The media has assisted in this public misconception, with most climate stories "balanced" with a "skeptic" perspective. However, this results in making the 2–3% seem like 50%. In trying to achieve "balance", the media has actually created a very unbalanced perception of reality. As a result, people believe scientists are still split about what's causing global warming, and therefore there is not nearly enough public support or motivation to solve the problem.

A critical thinker needs to decipher the elements of a news or media event before concluding that the presentation of facts and opinions has been balanced and completed with fairness.

LOGIC AND REASONING

Lurking behind all discussions of critical thinking and scientific analysis is familiarity with some basic principles of logic and reasoning. People reading research or scholars interpreting data can sometimes arrive at incorrect conclusions not only because of confirmation bias but also because of lapses in logic and reasoning. These principles are necessary tools to counteract misinformation and prevent opinion being pushed as fact. How often do we say something doesn't make sense, that it's not logical to hold a particular viewpoint, or that our interlocutor should stop being so unreasonable? *When hearing about, for example, climate change, UFO abductions, same-sex marriage, or psychic detectives, how much do you depend on logic to support arguments or question alternative positions?*

Let's look at some principles of logic with an example from a horoscope that appeared in a newspaper one day: "Scorpios are skeptical about horoscopes." What more could a critical thinker want to read? If you are skeptical about horoscopes, you would prove the horoscope true by announcing your skepticism—but then simultaneously you would be contradicting the horoscope, because you are now agreeing that it is accurately describing your views on horoscopes. This circular reasoning illustrates the importance of developing arguments that are inherently noncontradictory, that cannot be demonstrated to be false when carried out to extreme examples.

CRITICAL THINKING TIP

Apply the concepts and methods discussed in this book in everyday situations in order to discern the scams, misdirection, and obfuscations encountered. Use logic and reasoning to evaluate facts, to deduce or induce hypotheses, and to avoid the biases of opinion and faulty methodologies.

This simple statement captures the essence of one of the basic tenets of thought: Aristotle's *law of noncontradiction* and the absurdity of reducing something to its logical extreme. The law states that something cannot be true and not true at the same time; that would be absurd. It allows a person to ask how meaningful someone's position on an issue would be if it were taken to its logical extreme. Yet, making a reduction-to-the-absurd (*reductio ad absurdum*) argument can be an effective technique when refuting pseudoscientific statements and therefore one to consider adding to a repertoire of critical thinking tools.

Consider the use of this method by the mathematician John Allen Paulos, the author of *Innumeracy* (1989). In a December 13, 2009, *New York Times Magazine* article, he discussed the angered responses to a scientific panel's controversial advice that healthy women in their 40s should avoid routine mammograms until their 50s. Paulos argued that the public's reactions derived from an intuition that earlier screenings improve detection of a deadly cancer. However, he said that if this belief were true, then why not screen asymptomatic women in their 30s or, for that matter, beginning at age 15?

The panel's recommendations focused on the increased risk from cumulative radiation over many years outweighing the detection of cancer. Paulos (2009) demonstrates the use of the *reductio ad absurdum* technique to refute the common intuitive reaction in favor of the panel's more scientific findings. Whatever is true about one statement should then be true of similar statements based on the same premise, even when taken to the absurd limit. If it's accurate that earlier screening is better, then even earlier testing would be best. If not, then there is something logically incorrect about the initial statement that earlier is better. It is a proof by contradiction.

So how can these techniques and principles of logical thinking be useful for developing strong critical abilities? Review the following policy statement, similar to ones that have appeared with some regularity in the news: "Increasing taxes to allow all Americans to have health care will benefit the economy in the long run." Now take this to a logical extreme: Raising taxes to 100 percent of income should then bring about the best health care and a stronger economy! But devoting all of one's income to pay taxes would result in a failure to meet other obligations and purchase other goods, thereby bringing doom to the national economy and the health care system. Increasing taxes beyond a certain point contradicts the initial premise that better health care and a stronger economy result from raising taxes. The policy trick is to figure out what that certain point is and achieve a balance between necessary taxation and economic benefit.

If two statements contradict each other, they cannot both be true. Another example is the argument made by opponents to same-sex marriage who feel that legalizing it would harm the institution of marriage. Reducing this statement to the absurd, James Dobson of "Focus on the Family" predicted in 2004 (months after Massachusetts courts made these marriages legal) that same-sex marriage "will destroy marriage. It will destroy the Earth" (Wilson, 2011). *If you read or heard this comment, how would you respond logically—that is, with facts, not with just your opinion?*

The law of noncontradiction would have us believe that a state with legalized same-sex marriage would exhibit an increase in the dissolution of different-sex marriages and divorces, since the converse of Dobson's prediction (no impact or a strengthening of marriage) could not be equally true. In 2008, after four years of data, Massachusetts's divorce rate for heterosexual marriages declined from the previous year to the lowest level in the country and the lowest rate since 1940 (Wilson, 2011).

CRITICAL THINKING TIP

Engaging in a *reductio ad absurdum* and invoking the law of noncontradiction will assist you in critically thinking about people's arguments on current issues and in dealing with rumors that float around controversial policy plans. Seek out scientific evidence and actual data to provide much-needed assistance when evaluating reports and political arguments.

When confronted with dubious or pseudoscientific claims, Shermer (1997: 19) encourages a four-step process of skeptical thinking:

- *observation:* gather data;
- *induction:* draw conclusions from the data to formulate hypotheses;
- *deduction:* make predictions from the conclusions;
- *verification:* check the predictions with further observations and data.

Applying this process to the marriage topic: collect marriage and divorce data, draw conclusions (induce what same-sex marriage does to heterosexual marriages), predict (deduce with the null hypothesis) that legalizing same-sex marriage will not lead to increases in divorces, and verify with additional data over time.

When hearing or reading competing positions held by politicians and media pundits about controversial issues like health care, gun control, abortion, or solutions that promote our economic recovery, take their statements to logical extremes and uncover any potential contradictions. And use the logic of the four-step process of scientific inquiry and critical thinking to investigate and evaluate the claims. *How would you apply this four-step process to a dubious claim you recently read on a Facebook post or heard in the media?*

A FINAL CASE STUDY

Let's look at the role of reasoning, logic, facts, and opinions when confronting unusual situations, questionable research, and media reports by reviewing a well-known incident from the past. As you read this, ask yourself: *Could something like this happen today? What would be a modern equivalent in today's social media?*

On October 30, 1938, a now-infamous radio show put listeners' critical thinking skills to the test. According to a news bulletin that interrupted the supposed sounds of the Ramón Raquello Orchestra, live from the Meridian Room of the Park Plaza Hotel, Martians had landed in New Jersey and were running amok, destroying everything in sight.

In fact, CBS Radio was broadcasting a play based on H. G. Wells's *War of the Worlds*. It was not a fake news event, since the intention was to provide entertainment, not to purposely misinform. However, this version, Orson Welles's fiction, was interpreted as real news by many and resulted in panic around the country or, as *The New York Times* reported on the day after Halloween: "A wave of mass hysteria seized thousands of radio listeners between 8:15 and 9:30 o'clock last night." (Reproduced at www.war-of-the-worlds.org/Radio/Newspapers/Oct31 /NYT.html.)

Hadley Cantril's (1940) study of the psychology of panic, *The Invasion from Mars*, estimated that at least six million people, possibly as many as twelve million, tuned in to the show at some point that October evening. Of those, approximately 1.7 million listeners thought an invasion was really occurring, and 1.2 million of them panicked to some degree. As Glassner (1999: 205) asked: "Why do people embrace improbable pronouncements?"

One of the primary reasons for people's misunderstanding the show was tuning in late when they switched stations. Many had been listening to the rival top-rated show, ventriloquist Edgar Bergen and his Charlie McCarthy dummy, and missed the opening disclaimer that this was a fictional play of H. G. Wells's classic sci-fi novel. While demonstrating the power of specific social and psychological factors contributing to the panic, Cantril's research clearly pointed out the important role of critical thinking abilities in determining whether the show was a play or a live news event. *If a TV or radio show was interrupted with a warning about a major catastrophe, or you received a concerned text message from a friend or relative, what questions would you first ask to determine the reliability of the information?*

Using data from the American Institute of Public Opinion (led by the then-unknown George Gallup) and CBS Broadcasting's own survey, Cantril (1940) found that many listeners who used critical skills were not fooled; they analyzed internal evidence determining the event was not factual. For example, they recognized Orson Welles's distinctive voice, or figured that there was no way reporters could drive from New York City to distant parts of New Jersey within minutes of the first sightings to give a live on-the-air update. Others checked the newspaper to see "War of the Worlds" listed in the radio guide for that evening, turned to other stations and noticed it was not news there, or those living in New Jersey simply looked out the window to see whether there were fires and crowds of people streaming away from attacking Martians.

CRITICAL THINKING TIP

Healthy skepticism requires a foundation of relevant knowledge, logic, reasoning skills, and familiarity with the scientific methods necessary to achieve reliable and valid evidence. Ask what you would do today to determine whether a news story, Internet rumor, Facebook posting, text message, or e-mail solicitation is real, fictional, or a scam.

Yet, the power of selective perception and confirmation bias runs wild. As reported in Cantril's study, people who panicked tended to have personalities more prone to suggestion and susceptibility; they were often gullible and phobic worriers, religious and lower in self-confidence; and they tended to have poorer critical abilities.

For example, when determining whether the show was real by turning to another radio station, the panickers claimed to hear religious music: "I was sure a lot of people were worshiping God while waiting for their death." Or, upon hearing music said, "Nero fiddled while Rome burned." Others who looked out the window even had selective sensory responses: "I thought I could smell the gas. And it felt as though it was getting hot, like fire was coming." Most telling is this response from a frightened listener: "I knew it was some Germans trying to gas all of us. When the announcer kept calling them people from Mars, I just thought he was ignorant and didn't know yet that Hitler had sent them all."

And here we have the key sociopolitical reasons, besides fearful personalities, to explain why skeptical skills failed. We must keep in mind that critical thinking sometimes is put to the test even among the less phobic and more educated skeptical listeners. Social context can make a difference. People who were listening to the show without family members nearby or who were told to turn on the radio by scared neighbors or friends were more likely to panic, according to Cantril (1940).

Of course, in 1938, before television, most people kept up with the news about Hitler and Europe by listening to the radio. America was emerging from the Depression, and listeners with economic worries tended to be more susceptible to suggestion. Science-fiction comic strips and radio shows, media reports on the mysteries of science, and other advances in technology received regular public attention throughout the 1930s, and so stories of visitors from outer space seemed plausible to some listeners.

Developing critical ability and constructive skepticism clearly does not always inoculate us against moments of emotional panic, especially when the context is most threatening. Cantril (1940: 149) stated it well: "If critical ability is to be consistently exercised, it must be possessed by a person who is invulnerable in a crisis situation and who is impervious to extraneous circumstances."

A readiness to question interpretations with sufficient and relevant knowledge that's grounded in evidence, Cantril wrote, can lead to a healthy skepticism when confronting the challenging situations of daily life—and, as this book has demonstrated, when critically reading research and interpreting popular media reports of facts and opinions.

KEY TERMS

BALANCE The presentation of facts and information in a context that provides a sense of fairness and objectivity.

DEDUCTIVE REASONING Top-down logic going from a general theory to specific information, conclusions, and hypotheses.

FACTS Statements that are derived without bias from qualitative observations or quantitative evidence and that can be demonstrated to be true or false.

FAKE NEWS Stories purposely presented to misinform, as opposed to entertainment with humor; in certain political situations sometimes called propaganda.

INDUCTIVE REASONING Logic that begins with observations and concludes with a theory based upon them.

LAW OF NONCONTRADICTION Nothing can be both true and not true at the same time.

MISINFORMED (VERSUS UNINFORMED) Believing information that is false (versus not knowing information) about a topic.

OPINIONS Personal statements based on beliefs and emotions.

REDUCTIO AD ABSURDUM Argument in which a statement is disproved by its logically reaching an absurd conclusion.

EXERCISES

1. Go to the "opinion" section of the newspaper (online or print). Select an article and compare it with an article on the same issue that appears on the main news page. Explain how they differ in the following ways:
   (a) the content;
   (b) key phrases, words, sentences that signal an opinion or a fact;
   (c) photos, illustrations, and charts that reinforce the opinion or fact;
   (d) how much you learned about the topic;
   (e) how comprehensive and balanced the opinion and news article are;
   (f) how well either one helped you arrive at your own view of the topic.

2. Distinguish between fact and opinion. What elements help you decide in each of the following statements which is fact and which is opinion?
   (a) Students have a lot harder time in school than the teachers.
   (b) Popular music today is not as good as it was in the past.
   (c) It is illegal to yell out "Fire!" in a crowded movie theater.
   (d) People should not be allowed to talk on cell phones in a movie theater.

3. Seek out a recent news item that appeared on a fake news site. Find some at http://www.dailydot.com/layer8/fake-news-sites-list-facebook/:
   (a) Make a list of the key claims reported.
   (b) What evidence is provided for each of those claims?
   (c) Are any reliable sources quoted or research studies summarized?
   (d) What indicators suggest what you are reading is not factually authentic?

References

Agiesta, Jennifer. 2015 [Sept. 14]. "Misperceptions Persist about Obama's Faith, but Aren't So Widespread." *CNN.* http://www.cnn.com/2015/09/13/politics/barack-obama-religion-christian-misperceptions/index.html.

Agrawal, Nina. 2016 [Dec. 20]. "Where Fake News Came From—and Why Some Readers Believe It." *Los Angeles Times.* http://www.latimes.com/nation/la-na-fake-news-guide-2016-story.html.

van Agtmael, Peter. 2016 [May 12]. "Why Facts Aren't Always Truths in Photography." *Time.* http://time.com/4326791/fact-truth-photography-steve-mccurry/.

American Sociological Association. 2008. *ASA Code of Ethics.* Washington, D.C.: American Sociological Association. http://www.asanet.org/membership/code-ethics.

Americans United for Life. 2015 [June 24]. "AUL Releases *The New Leviathan:* The Mega-Centers Report, 'How Planned Parenthood Has Become Abortion, Inc.'" http://www.aul.org/2015/06/aul-releases-the-new-leviathan-the-mega-centers-report-how-planned-parenthood-has-become-abortion-inc/.

Assefi, Seema, and Maryanne Garry. 2003. "Absolut Memory Distortions: Alcohol Placebos Influence the Misinformation Effect." *Psychological Science* 14.1: 77–80.

Australian National Health and Medical Research Council. 2015. "NHMRC Statement on Homeopathy and NHMRC Information Paper—Evidence on the Effectiveness of Homeopathy for Treating Health Conditions." Canberra: National Health and Medical Research Council. http://www.nhmrc.gov.au/guidelines-publications/cam02.

Bao, Ying, et al. [Bao, Ying, Jiali Han, Frank B. Hu, Edward L. Giovannucci, Meir J. Stampfer, Walter C. Willett, and Charles S. Fuchs.] 2013. "Association of Nut Consumption with Total and Cause-Specific Mortality." *New England Journal of Medicine* 369: 2001–11.

Bausell, R. Barker. 2007. *Snake Oil Science: The Truth about Complementary and Alternative Medicine.* New York: Oxford University Press.

Bedard, Paul. 2013 [July 16]. "74% of Small Businesses Will Fire Workers, Cut Hours under Obamacare." *Washington Examiner.* http://www.washingtonexaminer.com/74-of-small-businesses-will-fire-workers-cut-hours-under-obamacare/article/2533131.

Belmont Report. 1979. "Ethical Principles and Guidelines for the Protection of Human Subjects of Research." Washington, D.C.: National Commission for the Protection of Human Subjects of Biomedical and Behavioral Research, U.S. Department of Health and Human Services. http://www.hhs.gov/ohrp/regulations-and-policy/belmont-report/#xethical.

Biesiekierski, Jessica, Jane Muir, and Peter Gibson. 2013. "Is Gluten a Cause of Gastrointestinal Symptoms in People without Celiac Disease?" *Current Allergy and Asthma Reports* 13.6: 631–38.

Billboard. 2014 [Nov. 19]. "Billboard 200 Makeover: Album Chart to Incorporate Streams & Track Sales." http://www.billboard.com/articles/columns/chart-beat/6320099/billboard-200-makeover-streams-digital-tracks.

Blumenthal, Mark. 2006 [Mar. 28]. "The AMA Spring Break Survey." *Mystery Pollster.* http://www.mysterypollster.com/main/2006/03/the_ama_spring_.html.

Broder, John. 2016 [Jan. 5]. "New Online Polling Experiment for the Post-Landline Phone Era." *New York Times.* http://www.nytimes.com/2016/01/05/insider/new-online-polling-experiment-for-the-post-landline-phone-era.html.

Browne, M. Neil, and Stuart Keeley. 2007. *Asking the Right Questions: A Guide to Critical Thinking.* 8th ed. New York: Pearson.

California Academy of Sciences. 2009 [Mar. 13]. "American Adults Flunk Basic Science." *ScienceDaily.* https://www.sciencedaily.com/releases/2009/03/090312115133.htm.

California Critical Thinking Skills Test-Numeracy. [CCTST-N.] 2016. *Insight Assessment.* San Jose, CA: California Academic Press. http://www.insightassessment.com/Products/Products-Summary/Critical-Thinking-Skills-Tests/California-Critical-Thinking-Skills-Test-Numeracy-CCTST-N.

California Highway Patrol. 2015. "New Study Shows Rising Use of Cell Phones While Driving." https://www.chp.ca.gov/PressReleases/Pages/New-Study-Shows-Rising-Use-of-Cell-Phones-While-Driving.aspx.

Cantril, Hadley. 1940. *The Invasion from Mars.* New York: Harper.

Carpenter, Susan. 2011 [Dec. 4]. "Young Adult Continues to Be the Literary World's Fastest-Growing Genre." *Los Angeles Times.* http://www.latimes.com/entertainment/la-ca-gift-guide-young-adult-20111204-story.html.

Carroll, Robert. 2003. *The Skeptic's Dictionary.* New York: Wiley. http://skepdic.com.

CAT. [Critical Thinking Assessment Test.] 2016. "Skills Assessed by CAT Instrument." Cookeville, TN: Tennessee Tech University. https://www.tntech.edu/cat/about/skills.

Centers for Disease Control and Prevention. 2016. "U.S. Public Health Service Syphilis Study at Tuskegee: The Timeline." http://www.cdc.gov/tuskegee/timeline.htm.

Chua, Amy, and Jed Rubenfeld. 2014. *The Triple Package: How Three Unlikely Traits Explain the Rise and Fall of Cultural Groups in America*. New York: Penguin.

CNN. 2016 [Nov. 9]. "Exit Polls: National President." http://www.cnn.com /election/results/exit-polls.

Davis, Matthew, Julie Bynum, and Brenda Sirovich. 2015. "Association between Apple Consumption and Physician Visits." *JAMA Internal Medicine* 175.5, 777–83.

De Langhe, Bart, Philip Fernbach, and Donald Lichtenstein. 2016. "Navigating the Stars: Investigating the Actual and Perceived Validity of Online User Ratings." *Journal of Consumer Research* 42.6, 817–33.

Deresiewicz, William. 2014 [Mar. 25]. "The Miseducation of the Tiger Mom." *New Republic*. https://newrepublic.com/article/117021/triple-package-amy-chua-and-jed-rubenfeld-reviewed.

Dolinar, Sean. 2014 [Sept. 19]. "Statistics—Probability vs. Odds." *Stats*. http:// stats.seandolinar.com/statistics-probability-vs-odds/.

Doyle, John. 2011 [Jan. 26]. "Psychic Nailed It." *New York Post*. http://nypost .com/2011/01/26/psychic-nailed-it/#ixzz1PIBmXpcq.

Ellie's Active Maths. 2011 [July 15]. "The Importance of Estimating." http:// activemaths.edublogs.org/2011/07/15/the-importance-of-estimating/.

Engel, Pamela. 2014 [Feb. 18]. "This Chart Shows an Alarming Rise in Florida Gun Deaths after 'Stand Your Ground' Was Enacted." *Business Insider.* http://www.businessinsider.com/gun-deaths-in-florida-increased-with-stand-your-ground-2014-2.

Ennis, Robert. 2015. *The Nature of Critical Thinking: Outlines of General Critical Thinking Dispositions and Abilities*. http://www.criticalthinking .net/longdefinition.html.

Ewald and Waserman Research Consultants. 2015. "Observational Study of Cell Phone and Texting Use among California Drivers 2015 and Comparison to 2011 through 2014." http://www.ots.ca.gov/pdf/2015-Cell-Phone-Observational-Survey.pdf

Forer, Bertram R. 1949. "The Fallacy of Personal Validation: A Classroom Demonstration of Gullibility." *The Journal of Abnormal and Social Psychology* 44.1: 118–23.

Freedberg, Louis. 2015 [Sept. 29]. "Teachers Say Critical Thinking Key to College and Career Readiness." *EdSource*. https://edsource.org/2015/teachers-say-critical-thinking-most-important-indicator-of-student-success/87810.

Friesen, Justin, Troy H. Campbell, and Aaron C. Kay. 2015."The Psychological Advantage of Unfalsifiability: The Appeal of Untestable Religious and Political Ideologies." *Journal of Personality and Social Psychology* 108.3: 515–29.

Frost, Jim. 2014 [Apr. 17]. "How to Correctly Interpret P Values." *The Minitab Blog*. http://blog.minitab.com/blog/adventures-in-statistics/how-to-correctly-interpret-p-values.

GAISE. [Guidelines for Assessment and Instruction in Statistics Education College Report.] 2015. *American Statistical Association*. http://www.amstat .org/education/gaise/GaiseCollege_Full.pdf.

Gallup. 2016. "How Does the Gallup Panel Work?" http://www.gallup .com/174158/gallup-panel-methodology.aspx.

Gavura, Scott. 2012 [July 5]. "Dr. Oz and Green Coffee Beans—More Weight Loss Pseudoscience." *Science-Based Medicine*. https://www.sciencebased medicine.org/dr-oz-and-green-coffee-beans-more-weight-loss-pseudoscience/.

Gawiser, Sheldon R., and G. Evans Witt. N.d. "20 Questions a Journalist Should Ask about Poll Results." *National Council on Public Polls*. http:// www.ncpp.org/?q = node/4.

Gilbert, Daniel, et al. [Gilbert, Daniel, Gary King, Stephen Pettigrew, and Timothy D. Wilson.] 2016. Comment on "Estimating The Reproducibility of Psychological Science." *Science* 351.6277: 1037.

Gilligan, Heather Tirado. 2015 [Apr. 12]. "Nutritional Science Isn't Very Scientific." *Slate*. http://www.slate.com/articles/life/food/2015/04/nutritional_ clinical_trials_vs_observational_studies_for_dietary_recommendations .html.

Glassner, Barry. 1999. *The Culture of Fear*. New York: Basic Books.

Goode, Erich. 2012. *The Paranormal: Who Believes, Why They Believe, and Why It Matters*. Amherst, NY: Prometheus Books.

GSS. [General Social Survey.] 2017. National Opinion Research Center, University of Chicago. http://gss.norc.org/.

Halpern, Diane. 1998. "Teaching Critical Thinking for Transfer across Domains." *American Psychologist* 53.4: 449–55.

Hamblin, James. 2014 [Jun. 18]. "Senators to Dr. Oz: Stop Promising Weight-Loss Miracles." *The Atlantic*. http://www.theatlantic.com/health/archive/2014 /06/magic-weight-loss-pills-may-not-exist/372958/.

Harris Interactive. 2013 [July 15]. "U.S. Chamber Releases Q2 Small Business Survey." https://www.uschamber.com/press-release/us-chamber-releases-q2- small-business-survey.

Hart, Joshua, and Christopher Chabris. 2016. "Does A 'Triple Package' of Traits Predict Success?" *Personality and Individual Differences* 94: 216–22.

Hart Research Associates. 2013. "It Takes More Than a Major: Employer Priorities for College Learning and Student Success." http://www.aacu.org /sites/default/files/files/LEAP/2013_EmployerSurvey.pdf.

Hickey, Walt. 2014 [Aug. 21]. "I Went To A Psychic and Then Found Out How Right She Really Was." *FiveThirtyEight*. http://fivethirtyeight.com/features /tarot-card-prediction-statistics/.

Hiebert, Paul. 2011 [Mar. 3]. "Our Obsession with the Word 'Random': Fear of a Millennial Planet." *The Awl*. https://theawl.com/our-obsession-with- the-word-random-fear-of-a-millennial-planet-bob4a0bbf38f.

Hines, Terence. 2003. *Pseudoscience and the Paranormal*. Amherst, NY: Prometheus Books.

Hodierne, Robert. 2009 [Feb.–Mar.]. "Is There Life after Newspapers?" *American Journalism Review*. http://ajrarchive.org/article.asp?id=4679.

Howard, Brian Clark. 2016 [Feb. 9]. "What Are the Odds a Meteorite Could Kill You?" *National Geographic*. http://news.nationalgeographic.com /2016/02/160209-meteorite-death-india-probability-odds/.

Huff, Darrell. 1954. *How to Lie with Statistics*. New York: Norton.

Jain, Anjali, Jaclyn Marshall, and Ami Buikema. 2015. "Autism Occurrence by MMR Vaccine Status among US Children with Older Siblings with and without Autism." *JAMA* 313.15: 1534–40.

Kaufman, Trent, Joshua Christensen, and Andrew Newton. 2015. "Employee Performance: What Causes Great Work?" *Cicero Group*. http://www .octanner.com/content/dam/oc-tanner/documents/white-papers/2015_Cicero_ WhitePaper_Drivers_of_Great_Work.pdf.

Kelly, I. W., J. Rotton, and R. Culver. 1996. "The Moon Was Full and Nothing Happened. A Review of Studies on the Moon and Human Behavior and Belief." In J. Nickell, B. Karr, and T. Genoni, eds., *The Outer Edge: Classic Investigations of The Paranormal*, 17–34. Amherst, NY: Committee for the Scientific Investigation of Claims of the Paranormal. [CSICOP].

Keohane, Joe. 2010 [July 11]. "How Facts Backfire." *Boston Globe*. http://archive .boston.com/bostonglobe/ideas/articles/2010/07/11/how_facts_backfire/.

Kida, Thomas. 2006. *Don't Believe Everything You Think: The 6 Basic Mistakes We Make in Thinking*. Amherst, NY: Prometheus Books.

Klinenberg, Eric. 2016 [Nov. 11]. "What Trump's Win Compels Scholars to Do." *Chronicle of Higher Education*. http://www.chronicle.com/article /What-Trump-s-Win-Compels/238389.

Koehler, Derek. 2016. "Can Journalistic 'False Balance' Distort Public Perception of Consensus in Expert Opinion?" *Journal of Experimental Psychology: Applied* 22.1: 24–38.

Kurtzleben, Danielle. 2015 [Aug. 4]. "Just How Arbitrary Is Fox's 10-Person GOP Debate Cutoff?" *NPR: National Public Radio*. http://www.npr.org /sections/itsallpolitics/2015/08/04/427711911/is-foxs-ten-person-gop-debate- cutoff-arbitrary.

LaCapria, Kim. 2016 [Feb. 18]. "Franzia Women Don't Get Fat." http://www .snopes.com/wine-makes-you-skinny/.

Leonard Lee, Shane Frederick, and Dan Ariely. 2006. "Try It, You'll Like It: The Influence of Expectation, Consumption, and Revelation on Preferences for Beer." *Psychological Science* 17.12: 1054–58.

Lepore, Jill. 2016 [Mar. 21]. "After the Fact." *The New Yorker*. http://www .newyorker.com/magazine/2016/03/21/the-internet-of-us-and-the-end-of-facts.

Leung, Angela Yee Man, et al. [Leung, Angela Yee Man, Ai Bo, Hsin-Yi Hsiao, Song Wang, and Iris Chi.] 2014. "Health Literacy Issues in the Care of Chinese American Immigrants with Diabetes: A Qualitative Study." *BMJ Open* 4.11. http://bmjopen.bmj.com/content/4/11/e005294.full.

Mayer-Schonberger, Viktor, and Kenneth Cukier. 2013. *Big Data: A Revolution That Will Transform How We Live, Work, and Think*. New York: Houghton Mifflin Harcourt.

MDK12.org. 2016. "School Improvement in Maryland: Data Interpretation." http://mdk12.msde.maryland.gov/instruction/curriculum/hsa/critical_think- ing/data_interpretation.html.

Miller, Jane. 2004. *The Chicago Guide to Writing about Numbers*. Chicago: University of Chicago Press.

Mitchell, Amy, et al. [Mitchell, Amy, Jeffrey Gottfried, Jocelyn Kiley, and Katerina Eva Matsa.] 2014. Political Polarization & Media Habits: Pew Research Center. http://www.journalism.org/2014/10/21/political-polarization-media-habits/.

Moore, Brooke Noel, and Richard Parker. 2009. *Critical Thinking*. 9th ed. New York: McGraw-Hill.

Nardelli, Alberto, and George Arnett. 2014 [Oct. 29]. "Today's Key Fact: You Are Probably Wrong about Almost Everything." *The Guardian*. http://www.theguardian.com/news/datablog/2014/oct/29/todays-key-fact-you-are-probably-wrong-about-almost-everything.

Nardi, Peter. 2014. *Doing Survey Research*. 3rd ed. New York: Routledge.

National Science Board. 2014. "Science and Technology: Public Attitudes and Understanding." Chapter 7 in *Science and Engineering Indicators*, pp. 7–1 to 7–53. https://www.nsf.gov/statistics/seind14/index.cfm/chapter-7/c7h.htm.

NBCNEWS.com. 2006 [Mar. 17]. "Girls Warned Not to 'Go Wild' on Spring Break." http://www.nbcnews.com/id/11726292/.

Newman, Mark. 2016. "Maps of the 2016 U.S. Presidential Election Results." Department of Physics and Center for the Study of Complex Systems, University of Michigan. http://www-personal.umich.edu/~mejn/election/2016/.

The News Manual. 2012. "Chapter 56: Facts and Opinion." http://www.thenewsmanual.net/Manuals%20Volume%203/volume3_56.htm.

Nisbett, Richard. 2015. *Mindware: Tools for Smart Thinking*. New York: Farrar, Straus and Giroux.

Nocera, Joe. 2016 [June 19]. "Screen Grab." *New York Times Magazine*, pp. 40–45, 52, 55, 57.

Novella, Steven. 2008 [Jan. 30]. "The Role of Anecdotes in Science-Based Medicine." *Science-Based Medicine*. https://www.sciencebasedmedicine.org/the-role-of-anecdotes-in-science-based-medicine/.

Nuccitelli, Dana. 2013 [May 16]. "Survey Finds 97% of Climate Science Papers Agree Warming Is Man-Made." *The Guardian*. https://www.theguardian.com/environment/climate-consensus-97-per-cent/2013/may/16/climate-change-scienceofclimatechange.

Nurses Health Study. [Brigham and Women's Hospital and Harvard T.H. Chan School of Public Health.] 2016. "About: History." http://www.nurseshealthstudy.org/about-nhs/history.

Nyhan, Brendan, and Jason Reifler. 2010. "When Corrections Fail: The Persistence of Political Misperceptions." *Political Behavior* 32: 303–30.

Open Science Collaboration. 2015. "Estimating the Reproducibility of Psychological Science." *Science* 349.6251: 943–51.

Oster, Emily. 2014 [Sept. 8]. "Don't Take Your Vitamins." *FiveThirtyEight*. http://fivethirtyeight.com/features/dont-take-your-vitamins/.

———. 2015 [Feb. 11]. "It's Hard to Know Where Gluten Sensitivity Stops and the Placebo Effect Begins." *FiveThirtyEight*. http://fivethirtyeight.com/features/its-hard-to-know-where-gluten-sensitivity-stops-and-the-placebo-effect-begins/.

Paul, Richard, Linda Elder, and Ted Bartell. 1997 [March]. "A Brief History of Critical Thinking." In *California Teacher Preparation for Instruction in Criti-*

cal Thinking: Research Findings and Policy Recommendations. Sacramento, CA: State of California, California Commission on Teacher Credentialing. [Reprinted in *The Critical Thinking Community*. http://www.criticalthinking .org/pages/a-brief-history-of-the-idea-of-critical-thinking/408.]

Paulos, John Allen. 1989. *Innumeracy: Mathematical Illiteracy and Its Conse-quences*. New York: Hill and Wang.

———. 2009 [Dec. 13]. "Mammogram Math." *New York Times Magazine*. http://www.nytimes.com/2009/12/13/magazine/13Fob-wwln-t.html.

Pérez-Peña, Richard. 2015 [Sept. 21]. "1 in 4 Women Experience Sex Assault on Campus." *New York Times*. http://www.nytimes.com/2015/09/22/us/a-third-of-college-women-experience-unwanted-sexual-contact-study-finds. html.

Pew Research Center. 2014 [Feb. 4]. "6 New Facts about Facebook." http:// www.pewresearch.org/fact-tank/2014/02/03/6-new-facts-about-facebook/.

———. 2015a [June 11]. "Multiracial in America: Proud, Diverse and Growing in Numbers." http://www.pewsocialtrends.org/2015/06/11/multiracial-in-america/.

———. 2015b [Aug. 6]. "Teens, Technology and Friendships: Methods." http:// www.pewinternet.org/2015/08/06/methods-34/.

———. 2015c [Oct. 19]. "Slightly Fewer Americans Are Reading Print Books, New Survey Finds." http://www.pewresearch.org/fact-tank/2015/10/19 /slightly-fewer-americans-are-reading-print-books-new-survey-finds/.

———. 2015d [Apr. 9]. "Teens, Social Media & Technology Overview 2015." http://www.pewinternet.org/2015/04/09/teens-social-media-technology-2015/.

———. 2016a. "U.S. Survey Research: Sampling." http://www.pewresearch .org/methodology/u-s-survey-research/sampling/.

———. 2016b. "News Use across Social Media Platforms 2016." http:// www.journalism.org/2016/05/26/news-use-across-social-media-platforms-2016/.

Postman, Neil, and Charles Weingartner. 1969. *Teaching as a Subversive Activ-ity*. New York: Dell Delta.

Qui, Linda. 2015 [Oct. 1]. "Chart Shown at Planned Parenthood Hearing Is Misleading and 'Ethically Wrong.'" *Politifact*. http://www.politifact.com /truth-o-meter/statements/2015/oct/01/jason-chaffetz/chart-shown-planned-parenthood-hearing-misleading-/.

Radford, Ben. 2011 [Apr. 14]. "Psychic Tip on Long Island Serial Killer?" *Seeker*. http://www.seeker.com/psychic-tip-on-long-island-serial-killer-1765214460 .html.

Rhodes, Terrel, ed. 2010a. "Critical Thinking VALUE Rubric." Excerpted from *Assessing Outcomes and Improving Achievement: Tips and Tools for Using Rubrics*. Washington, D.C.: Association of American Colleges and Universi-ties. https://www.aacu.org/value/rubrics/critical-thinking.

———. 2010b. "Quantitative Literacy VALUE Rubric." Excerpted from *Assessing Outcomes and Improving Achievement: Tips and Tools for Using Rubrics*. Washington, D.C.: Association of American Colleges and Universi-ties. http://www.aacu.org/value/rubrics/quantitative-literacy.

Robinson, Nicola. 1999. "The Use of Focus Group Methodology—with Selected Examples from Sexual Health Research." *Journal of Advanced Nursing* 29.4: 905–13.

Roithmayr, Daria. 2014 [Feb. 12]. "The Flaw at the Heart of *The Triple Package*." *Slate*. http://www.slate.com/articles/health_and_science/books/2014/02/amy_chua_and_jed_rubenfeld_s_the_triple_package_reviewed.html.

Rosenthal, Jack. 2006 [Aug. 27]. "Precisely False vs. Approximately Right: A Reader's Guide to Polls." *New York Times*. http://www.nytimes.com/2006/08/27/opinion/27pubed.html.

Sagan, Carl. 1987. "The Burden of Skepticism." *Skeptical Inquirer* 12.1. http://www.csicop.org/si/show/burden_of_skepticism.

Saulny, Susan. 2011 [Mar. 19]. "Black and White and Married in the Deep South: A Shifting Image." *New York Times*. http://www.nytimes.com/2011/03/20/us/20race.html.

Shermer, Michael. 1997. *Why People Believe Weird Things: Pseudoscience, Superstition, and Other Confusions of Our Time*. New York: Freeman.

Silverman, Craig. 2016 [Nov. 16]. "This Analysis Shows How Fake Election News Stories Outperformed Real News on Facebook." *BuzzFeed News*. https://www.buzzfeed.com/craigsilverman/viral-fake-election-news-outperformed-real-news-on-facebook.

SPSS. 2017. "IBM SPSS Statistics Base." http://www-03.ibm.com/software/products/en/spss-stats-base.

Squire, Peverill. 1988. "Why the 1936 *Literary Digest* Poll Failed." *Public Opinion Quarterly* 52.1: 125–33.

Stabile, Matt. 2016 [Dec. 11]. "How Many Americans Have A Passport?" *The Expeditioner*. http://www.theexpeditioner.com/2010/02/17/how-many-americans-have-a-passport-2/.

Steen, Lynn Arthur, and the Quantitative Literacy Design Team. 2001. "The Case for Quantitative Literacy." In *Mathematics and Democracy: The Case for Quantitative Literacy*, ed. Lynn Arthur Steen, 1–12. Princeton: National Council on Education and the Disciplines. http://www.maa.org/sites/default/files/pdf/QL/MathAndDemocracy.pdf.

This American Life. 2001 [June 8]. "Prom." Transcript, episode 186. http://www.thisamericanlife.org/radio-archives/episode/186/transcript.

Timmer, John. 2006 [Oct. 13]. "Scientists on Science: Tentativeness." *Ars Technica*. http://arstechnica.com/science/2006/10/5609/.

Tremblay, Pierre, and Nadège Sauvêtre. 2014. "'Jockeys and Joyriders' Revisited: Young Offenders' Involvement in Motor Vehicle Thefts in the Province of Quebec." *Canadian Journal of Criminology and Criminal Justice* 56.2: 167–83.

Tufte, Edward. 2001. *The Visual Display of Quantitative Information*. 2nd ed. Cheshire, CT: Graphics Press.

United States Census Bureau. 2015. "Quick Facts." http://www.census.gov/quickfacts/table/LFE305214/00.

United States Chamber of Commerce. 2013 [July 15]. "U.S. Chamber Releases Q2 Small Business Survey." https://www.uschamber.com/press-release/us-chamber-releases-q2-small-business-survey.

Valverde, Miriam. 2016 [Oct. 31]. Pants on Fire! Trump Says Clinton Would Let 650 Million People into the U.S., in One Week." *Politifact.* http://www.politifact.com/truth-o-meter/statements/2016/oct/31/donald-trump/trump-says-clinton-would-bring-650-million-people-/.

Vigen, Tyler. 2015. *Spurious Correlations.* New York: Hachette. http://tylervigen.com/spurious-correlations.

VinePair. 2015 [July 1]. "Wine as a Bedtime Snack Helps with Weight Loss." http://vinepair.com/booze-news/wine-as-a-bedtime-snack-helps-with-weight-loss/.

Vinson, Joe, Bryan Burnham, and Mysore Nagendran. 2012. "Randomized, Double-Blind, Placebo-Controlled, Linear Dose, Crossover Study to Evaluate the Efficacy and Safety of a Green Coffee Bean Extract in Overweight Subjects." *Diabetes, Metabolic Syndrome and Obesity: Targets and Therapy* 5: 21–27. http://www.ncbi.nlm.nih.gov/pmc/articles/PMC4206203/. [Retracted in 2014.]

Wade, Lisa. 2014 [Dec. 28]. "How to Lie with Statistics: Stand Your Ground and Gun Deaths." *Sociological Images.* https://thesocietypages.org/socimages/2014/12/28/how-to-lie-with-statistics-stand-your-ground-and-gun-deaths/.

Wang, Lu, et al. [Wang, Lu, I-Min Lee, JoAnn E. Manson, Julie E. Buring, and Howard D. Sesso.] 2010. "Alcohol Consumption, Weight Gain, and Risk of Becoming Overweight in Middle-aged and Older Women. *Archives of Internal Medicine* 70.5: 453–61.

Wartberg, Lutz, et al. [Wartberg, Lutz, Rudolf Kammerl, Moritz Rosenkranz, Lena Hirschhauser, Sandra Hein, Christiane Schwinge, Kay-Uwe Petersen, and Rainer Thomasius.] 2014. "The Interdependence of Family Functioning and Problematic Internet Use in a Representative Quota Sample of Adolescents." *Cyberpsychology, Behavior, and Social Networking* 17.1: 14–18.

Wilson, Bruce. 2011 [May 25]. "Divorce Rate in Gay Marriage–Legal MA Drops to Pre-WWII Level." *The Huffington Post.* http://www.huffingtonpost.com/bruce-wilson/divorce-rate-in-gay-marri_b_267259.html.

Wingfield, Nick, Mike Isaac, and Katie Benner. 2016 [Nov. 14]. "Google and Facebook Take Aim at Fake News Sites." *New York Times.* http://www.nytimes.com/2016/11/15/technology/google-will-ban-websites-that-host-fake-news-from-using-its-ad-service.html.

Wiseman, Richard, and Donald West. 1996. "An Experimental Test of Psychic Detection." *Journal of the Society for Psychical Research* 61.842: 34–45.

World Bank Group. 2014. "World Development Indicators: Health Systems." http://wdi.worldbank.org/table/2.15.

World Factbook. 2015. "Total Fertility Rate" Washington, D.C.: Central Intelligence Agency. https://www.cia.gov/library/publications/the-world-factbook/fields/2127.html#.

World Health Organization. 2013. "World Health Statistics 2013." http://www.who.int/gho/publications/world_health_statistics/EN_WHS2013_Full.pdf.

Zuckerman, Ezra, and John Jost. 2001. "What Makes You Think You're So Popular? Self-Evaluation Maintenance and the Subjective Side of the 'Friendship Paradox.'" *Social Psychology Quarterly* 64.3: 207–23.

Index

A/B testing, 123, 124
alternative explanations, 6, 8, 11, 98–103, 104, 108, 112, 117–18; antecedent, 102; intervening, 102; spurious, 100, 102; suppressing, 102
anecdotes, 1, 14, 33–35, 44, 108–9, 112, 113, 114, 124, 131

Big Data, 58, 96, 122–23, 125, 128

causality (causation), 14, 15, 34, 92–104, 108, 122; necessary and sufficient, 93. *See also* correlation
central tendency measures, 23–27; average, 13, 21, 23, 24, 26, 28, 29, 53, 120; mean, 24–26, 30, 31; median, 25–26, 29, 30, 31, 60; mode, 26, 27, 30; standard deviation, 24–25, 30
charts. *See* visualization
coincidence, 10, 53–55, 61
confidence interval. *See* margin of error
confirmation bias, 54, 61, 109, 125, 130, 131, 134, 140
control group, 107, 118–21, 125
control variable. *See* alternative explanations
correlation, 58, 92, 94–95, 96, 104; and causation, 10, 92–105, 109, 122
critical thinking, 5–8; and cynicism, 4; Greek roots, 5, 7; and skepticism, 4, 138, 141

Critical Thinking Assessment Test (CAT), 6–7, 9, 10, 11
critical thinking tips, 12, 16, 18, 19, 22, 23, 26, 28, 35, 39, 42, 46, 54, 56, 58, 67, 70, 74, 76, 78, 86, 95, 96, 98, 101, 109, 110, 111, 116, 117, 119, 122, 129, 133, 136, 138, 140
cross-sectional, 97, 104, 113, 118, 121
crosstabs (contingency tables), 82–86, 88

double-blind. *See* experiments

ecological fallacy, 37, 48
estimation, 27–29, 60; and rounding off, 28
ethics, 45–48; anonymity versus confidentiality, 47, 48; autonomy, 47; Belmont Report, 47; beneficence, 47; informed consent, 45, 46, 48; institutional review board (IRB), 46, 48; justice, 47; miscalculations, 18; Tuskegee Study of Untreated Syphilis, 45–46. *See also* fairness and balance
evidence, 4, 8, 34, 94, 108, 110, 112, 114, 116, 124, 128–29, 131, 133, 139, 141. *See also* fact
experiments, 14, 108, 118–21; case-controlled design, 121, 125; cohort prospective design, 122, 125; randomized double-blind placebo control (RDBPC), 107, 118–19, 121, 124, 125

CPSIA information can be obtained
at www.ICGtesting.com
Printed in the USA
LVHW01s0212030818
585752LV00005B/1004/P